LIVING IN TIME
A New Look at Personal Development

Phillida Salmon

J. M. DENT & SONS LTD
London and Melbourne

First published 1985
© Phillida Salmon, 1985

This book is set in 11/13pt Linotron Plantin by
Inforum Ltd, Portsmouth

Printed in Great Britain for
J. M. Dent & Sons Ltd
Aldine House, 33 Welbeck Street, London W1M 8LX

British Library Cataloguing in Publication Data

Salmon, Phillida
   Living in time.
   1. Developmental psychology   2. Social
   psychology
   I. Title
   155   BF713

ISBN 0-460-02280-6

CONTENTS

1 INTRODUCTION

How do people come to change as time goes on? How is it that individuals come to be so different from each other? These are fundamental human questions with which all of us are, in some sense, concerned. Whether we are coping with a new baby, struggling with a difficult pupil, supporting a friend through a crisis, or reflecting on the course our own life has taken – our interest in such questions is not just academic, but personal and vital.

As a developmental psychologist, I have a special interest in these questions. For many years now I have been teaching developmental psychology, to people taking psychology degrees, in-service courses for teachers, classes in adult education. Among those who organize such courses, who prepare the texts and materials for them, there is a high degree of agreement as to how they should be constituted. In studying the subject, it is expected that people will trace the normal course of human development, learn the milestones along the way, discover the personal changes which each new phase should introduce.

The first thing which, in courses like these, any student learns is that development in human life stops short. The subject ends its story at the early twenties. By that stage, it is assumed, human beings are complete. Whatever particularities, whatever idiosyncrasies that, as people, they possess, will have been permanently established by the end of their teenage years. Adult life is not seen, in this account, as properly developmental, and is therefore not included as belonging in the syllabus. As for late human life, this is treated by psychologists as a special subject on its own: the psychology of ageing. This subject is, in a basic way, the mirror image of developmental psychology. Its material, too, consists of the personal changes of human beings; but they are changes of regression, of decline, of deterioration.

All this, perhaps, seems just what one would expect. The idea that, during childhood and youth, we gradually come to maturity, that, in our adult years, we maintain a steady course without radical changes, and that during old age, we begin, personally, to decline – surely this is no more than common knowledge? Most people who, for whatever reason, begin to study psychology, are not particularly surprised by what they find, since, basically, the content of the subject confirms what they knew already.

The close agreement between official psychology and conventional wisdom is something we should think about. Psychology, as an academic subject, is not like chemistry. Psychologists are themselves people, representatives of their own subject matter. And since, as people, they breathe the same air as other people – are subject to the same social constraints and expectations, assimilate the same assumptions, the same prejudices – perhaps in their academic pronouncements, they give scientific respectability to what is basically only 'common knowledge'.

This is not at all how we generally regard psychology. Surely, as a science, it uses methods which properly establish what is really the case, which distinguish impartially between truth and falsehood? Do not these methods, based on logic and statistics, put its findings altogether beyond dispute?

One way of reflecting on this question is to consider something of the changes, over recent years, in official psychology. One instance is the construction of tests of 'intelligence'. When 'intelligence tests' came into widespread use, during the first part of this century, their 'norms', against which people's answers were measured, were such that men and women, boys and girls, characteristically ended up with different 'Intelligence Quotients'. Males, of whatever age, tended to do better, to score, on these tests, as more 'intelligent' than females. This 'finding' was regarded as altogether unsurprising; it fitted with current social assumptions, which saw men, but not women, as intellectually equipped to vote. It was only later, when social movements like those of the Suffragettes had forced a reconsideration of the position of women, that psychologists began to question the intellectual superiority, built into their measuring instruments, of males over females. Only as members of a society itself obliged to rethink the meaning of gender, did psychologists come to view the 'norms' they had been using as biased, and to restandardize their tests so that males and females would achieve a similar range of scores. Nor does the current situation represent any final 'truth'; perhaps future generations will view the norms used today as incorporating their own kinds of bias.

If the construction of supposedly objective psychological instruments was, in this way, drastically influenced by current assumptions about male-female comparability, then perhaps today's 'scientific' pronouncements about the life cycle are equally open to the prevailing social ethos. Ours is a society which marks off its members by chronological age, and which gives a differential significance to early and late time. The official account of psychology creates essential discontinuities between childhood, adulthood and old age, and thereby reflects social practices which relegate both the old and the young to special institutions, separated from the mainstream of human affairs. Living in a social context where youth is generally courted and admired, old age, treated with fear and disrespect, psychologists have produced a story of the life cycle where positive value is accorded only to the first part.

Developmental psychology does, in this, lend its own kind of validity to a philosophy of life which is embedded in many of our habitual assumptions. It is a philosophy which, at its crudest, was expressed in a recent radio interview by the editor of a fashionable and influential magazine, *Cosmopolitan*.* The only real goals of human life, she maintained, could be sex, money and success. Age, conversely, was 'a disease to be fought every inch of the way'. Sex, money, success – if these are available, it is more likely to be during adulthood, rather than in childhood or old age. In defining the adult years as the apex of life, in seeing the value of

* Brown, H. G., *In the Psychiatrist's Chair*, BBC Radio 4 interview, 18 August 1984.

childhood only as a progression towards adulthood, psychology seems to be endorsing the same kind of philosophy. And by portraying old age as a time of personal decline, of human deterioration, psychology echoes the same sense of hostility and dread, and acts to justify all the institutional practices which exclude elderly people from the mainstream of human life.

Not every psychologist, of course, would accept the portrayal of human life which I have been describing; there are occasional voices raised which express very different views. But the consensus in psychology does essentially define the life cycle in terms of discontinuity, of the differential value of particular phases, of positive early changes and negative later ones, and of the central period of life as an unchanging plateau. When the picture offered is one which accords so well with our conventional wisdom, when all that it describes is visibly borne out by what we see when we look around us – it is very difficult, in this situation, to challenge the assumptions of psychology. And given the enormous respect which most people feel for 'science', it is perhaps not surprising that few of us would venture to dispute what is presented as objectively, scientifically, established.

Yet surely it is essential to examine the philosophy by which we live. As long as we go on accepting the received wisdom, refusing to question habitual assumptions, we shall continue to live out what may ultimately be a demeaning, an impoverishing philosophy of human life. We shall blindly endorse the particular forms and practices of our own society, despite the diminution, the disrespect, which these incorporate for certain phases, certain lives. It is because, as human beings, we do live out what we take to be true – we create the reality in which we believe – that our psychology is not just something for academic study, but the very underpinning of the way we live.

How should we set about examining our psychology, our ideas about the human life cycle, our sense of the courses that our lives should take? It must first be necessary to look, as carefully as we can, at the main phases of human life. If we consider what it means to be a child, an old person, an adult, living in our society, what conclusions shall we come to? Shall we find that there are basic qualitative differences between these phases of life – that, as human beings, children are fundamentally different from grownups, and that, on their side, elderly people are distinctive, different kinds of people? Or shall we see human existence as basically continuous, and human beings as retaining their own kind of personhood as they travel through their lives?

Centrally built into the understanding we have of the course of our development is the idea of normality. We assume that childhood, adulthood, old age should take particular forms. People whose development conforms to these patterns we call normal, and, by the same token, we define as deviant those whose life courses depart from these patterns. The developmental consequences of such definitions, at any life stage, can themselves be massive. Through more than a decade of work as a clinical psychologist, I saw for myself how the diagnosis of personal deviance, and the institutional provision to which it leads, may entail a diminution of humanity granted to those involved. It is surely vital, therefore, to look at our assumptions about what is the proper course that life should take. And perhaps, if we can momentarily suspend our horror, our dismay, at lives which depart from conventional patterns, we may enlarge our own sense of humanity.

In examining questions like these, we necessarily become aware of how much our judgments about human life depend upon our dealings with each other. Throughout our lives we achieve our sense of what things mean by the mutual references we constantly make. Our psychology arises out of our social consensus, is confirmed by the social transactions in which we are involved. The meaning we give to human development, to the course of human life, is itself socially negotiated. To realize this is to see the particular forms which life generally takes in our own society, not as fixed and immutable, but as historically and culturally relative – as open, potentially, to social reconstruction, to the development of other, perhaps richer forms.

If we are to stand back from our habitual ways of understanding, buttressed as they are by the claims of official psychology, we shall need to separate out the various strands that make up our explanation of why people develop as they do. When we think about how it is that, even in the 'same' environment, different people grow up differently, it is to gender that, above all, we turn. At every phase of human life, males and females are differentiated. In their growth as people, boys and girls are headed for different sorts of developmental goals. And from the earliest months of life, most people, most official psychology, would say, the differential human destiny carried by gender is clear and obvious. This destiny, we generally think, is present within our genetic inheritance, and unless we encounter major disabling experiences during childhood, we shall simply live it out. Yet gender, if we look closely at it, may turn out to mean something rather different. Again, we shall need to pay attention to all the ways in which – even for this apparently inbuilt difference – we act together to construct its meaning in our lives as human beings.

Our understanding of human development also rests upon a certain view of physical growth and physical functioning. We see childhood and youth as representing positive movement – changes that are essentially progressive. In this, it seems obvious and natural to identify psychological with physical development. Just as their bodies grow steadily stronger, more agile, with the years, so, we believe, children gradually develop all the skills, all the understanding that, as adults, they will possess. And the converse, we assume, applies in old age. As her body becomes ever more decrepit, more infirm, so the old woman increasingly shows signs of human decay – becomes forgetful, petulant, childish. At both early and late stages of life, we equate bodily changes with personal ones. And during the years of adulthood, in which fewer physical changes occur, we assume that people remain basically static, unchanging. In thinking about human development, it will be necessary to consider, as far as we can, the human meaning of our physical embodiment. Again, the relation between people and their bodies may seem, on reflection, to be altogether less crude, and less fixed, than we generally think.

In how we understand the mechanisms, the processes, of human development, we give weight to certain aspects, stress particular factors in our lives. Conventional wisdom and official psychology are generally agreed that, during childhood, people become permanently, irreversibly moulded. In this, it is the family which is seen as having supreme importance. It is, we generally suppose, the experience of growing up in a 'normal' family that produces people who are basically all right. Conversely, to grow up in families which are atypical or unstable in pattern, or families where child-rearing does not take a conventional form – this is to suffer basic and irrevocable damage to one's development as a human being. In examining these assumptions, we must try to see what family life generally means for people in our society – for adults as well as for children. It may be that, to understand the immense significance for most people of their experience in families, we should view it in other terms from those we generally employ. The impact, on later life, of early family life, may be less that of producing an individual shape that can never afterwards be altered, than that of providing certain basic terms in which experience can be cast, and life lived.

A further aspect of our lives which, in reflecting on our own developmental psychology, we shall need to include, has to do with the experience of loss. This feature of human life is something about which the official psychology of development has very little to say; and, because it is essentially painful, most of us do not readily approach it. Yet an understanding of its meaning is present in the way we view the life cycle, if only by implication. It is because we see youth as a time in which things are *acquired* – skills, achievements, property, social status, personal relationships – that we define it as a period of development, of positive growth. And it is because, as we generally believe, all these things are gradually *lost* during old age, that this phase is seen as one of negative growth, of regression. Yet if we try to consider what human loss essentially entails, we may come to see it differently. It may be that loss is an inescapable part of every life phase, that, for children, for adult men and women, just as for elderly people, human beings must lose what they love. Perhaps, though, there are ways of experiencing loss which render it more than simply negative – which are, in themselves, humanly developing.

If we are to do full justice to the exploration of our own developmental psychology, we shall need to enter the ground of metaphor. We do not usually think of ourselves as using metaphors, except when we are being particularly fanciful or poetic. We generally believe that we experience things as they literally are, without the interposition of another level of meaning. Yet in the end, it is through the metaphorical interpretations we place upon the life cycle that we come to experience the deepest meanings of our lives. Perhaps you see your life course as a journey, which has its own direction, signposts, choice points, its own kind of progression. Or you may experience your life as a moral trial, in which your human worth is put to a life-long test, so that, in the end, you may be personally judged. It is the metaphorical account which, basically and intuitively, we make of our lives which gives them, ultimately, the significance they have.

So, in considering the psychology we have constructed, and might construct, about the meaning of development, we shall need to examine the profound influence of metaphor. In this, it may be illuminating to look at three metaphorical accounts, which have distinctive, very different perspectives on the life cycle.

Developmental psychology is, finally, a way of understanding what time means in human life. In our usual view, we represent time as having a standard significance. We see it as operating in a fixed and inevitable way – as ushering in, through chronological age, human changes that are wanted or unwanted. We view time as essentially linear – as going in one direction only. All this is, perhaps, open to question. We may find, if we give the issue full and careful consideration, that our experience of time is far more complex, far more delicate, than we usually allow. And since, in the last analysis, our developmental psychology is our understanding of living in time, it is with the question of time itself that we should begin.

2 EXPERIENCING TIME

Among more than 16,000 items in the *Oxford Dictionary of Quotations*, references to time outnumber all others except those to man, woman, child, life, death and love. As an index of the sayings that people have found to be striking, memorable or illuminating, this suggests that time has been, and remains, an enduring focus of human preoccupation. In this chapter, I want to consider some questions about why time is so important to us, how time is generally experienced, and what time seems to mean in human lives.

One way of reflecting on what is involved in time, is to imagine what it would be like if the passing of time could not be marked. This is something that happens in a story by Sylvia Townsend Warner – *Mr Fortune's Maggot*. Mr Fortune, a would-be missionary who is instead converted to paganism, forgets to rewind his watch during the hurricane which devastates the island where he is living. The impact of this small incident undermines his psychological stability far more than the other, much greater losses he suffers.

Disconsolately he looked at his watch. It had stopped. In the stress of overnight he had forgotten to wind it up, and now it recorded the epoch at which his last link with European civilization had been snapped – eight hours thirty-five minutes. It could not be much later than that now. But a miss is as good as a mile, and for the rest of his sojourn on the island, for the rest of his life maybe, he would not know what o'clock it was. This circumstance, not serious in itself and not to be compared with the loss of the medicine chest or his books, upset him horribly. He felt frightened, he felt as small and desperate as a child lost. 'I must set it as best I can,' he thought. . . . At last he settled on ten-twenty-five; but even so he still delayed, for he felt a superstitious reluctance to move the hands and so destroy the last authentic witness his watch could bear him. Five minutes, he judged, had been spent in this weak-minded dallying: so resolutely he set the hands to ten-thirty and wound the poor machine up. It began to tick, innocently, obediently. It had set out on its fraudulent career.*

For Mr Fortune, as perhaps for all of us, time and its passing represent a vital anchor in defining ourselves and our lives – an anchor without which we are totally at sea. Only in marking the passage of the years, the days, the hours, can we feel we are retaining a firm hold on stable reality. This itself is paradoxical. The essence of time is that it brings change; it alters things, it ushers in what is new and unpredictable. Yet, despite this, somehow it is time itself which provides us with a fundamental sense of security.

When we consciously reflect on time and what it means for us, it is to its transience, its mutability, that we generally turn. This involves the sense of the inexorability of time passing – what Conrad called 'the remorseless rush of time'. One inescapable part of that remorseless rush is the fact of loss: a theme which has profound resonances for most people, and which is central to much enduring literature. All of us, from young childhood on, know what it is to lose the things we love. With Alain-Fournier,† we can look back wistfully, longingly, to the lost domain we once knew. Like Tennyson, we can yearn for the touch of a vanished hand, the sound of a voice that is still. At times, such feelings can cast their shadow over all that is our life now: 'change and decay in all around I see'.

But time does not only mean change and loss; it also means continuity. In marking the passing of the years, we make our

* Warner, S. Townsend, *Mr Fortune's Maggot*, Virago, 1978.
† Alain-Fournier, *Le Grand Meaulnes*, trans. Penguin Modern Classics, 1966.

lives continuous with those who have lived before us – and by this means, partly overcome their transience, their littleness. Time is also fundamental in the way we establish a sense of stability in our everyday lives. It is by defining our days as *un*changing that we can feel confident in living them. The repetition of the diurnal cycle, the hours by which we count it and through which we regulate what we do – these things persuade us of the solid reality, the predictability of our everyday worlds. In this way, we define time in terms of the recurrence of what is familiar, and thereby reassure ourselves of the continuity of our lives. If we lose this, we lose our hold on reality. The imaginary Mr Fortune's sense of catastrophe, in not knowing the 'right' time, is echoed in the actuality of people's urgent concern, after suffering a stroke or other brain injury, to know how many days have passed since the last events they remember.

In human life, time is also the essential mode through which we affirm the durability of what is deeply significant. The days which we make 'special' represent this kind of affirmation. Public commemorative days – Christmas, New Year's Day, Armistice Day – celebrate the permanence of values which are supposedly shared by everyone in our society. Birthdays or wedding anniversaries are occasions when family groups affirm the abiding significance for their members of the birth or the marriage involved. In voluntary groupings, annual reunions serve to assert the continuing personal importance and meaningfulness of the grouping, and the events out of which it grew. Sometimes individuals have their own private special days, in which, in one way or another, they mark the significance of the particular events. And these occasions can be much more than merely rituals. The day on which people die can be the day on which a loved parent also died.

Not only do we use time to mark what, in a sense, transcends time. As human beings, we also feel our lives, our selves, to be time-marked. In its widest scope, this entails the sense of living in history. It is rare, perhaps, to experience this sense more than momentarily. Sometimes, in childhood, one has a sudden brief revelation. These stones, these very stones I am now standing on, have actually been trodden on by the feet of real people who lived hundreds of years ago. For a moment, the stones take on an utterly different quality – and then they revert to being ordinary stones in the ordinary present. In adult life, a sense of living in the time-scale of history seems usually just as evanescent. Some people glimpse distant future time as they try to envisage the lives of grandchildren and great-grandchildren. Or sometimes, the situation of parenthood is experienced as a recapitulation of one's own parents' parenthood. At such moments, people can feel themselves to be identified not merely with their own parents, but with all the myriads of other parents who have lived before them, and will live after them. Sometimes, too, the realization of living in history comes through the sense of having been a part of 'great events' – of having oneself been one of the small strands in those events. It may be, though, that this dimension of experience is less readily available to some people in our society than to others. As 'History' is constituted, its landmarks overwhelmingly reflect the concerns, the activities, of men. Women in our society, whose lives are much less historically scripted, may not so easily experience a sense of oneness with earlier lives through such publicly commemorated events.

Yet perhaps for everyone, there are moments when we realize, with a sudden shock, that we have a personal past which is itself history. Seeing a snapshot of oneself at an earlier time can bring strong and complicated feelings. There we stand, confidently embedded in *that* present, entirely unaware of how old-fashioned, how quaint, we look. That is *us*, yet what an unbridgeable distance separates that person from the person living now! That young face, so familiar, yet so strange, has gone for ever. Even children can feel this, as they stare at an earlier self with disbelieving recognition.

Revelations that time has worked changes in us can also arise out of our relations with others. A child's amazement in discovering that she understands the principles of computer programming, say, better than her father can be exciting, but also disturbing. It conveys something of a hugely significant shift in her own position, as a member of the younger generation, towards members of an older generation. In adult life, there is sometimes a sudden, uncomfortable lurch into awareness of how old we 'really' are. The taken-for-granted assumption of being one of the group is unexpectedly swept away by the realization that, to the others, you represent an older and different generation. Or conversely, you find, with consternation, that for all those old people, you are another old person, one of them. Sometimes, the time-marking of ourselves, by us or by others, arises in noticing that our personal tastes, personal style, seem to crystallize those of an earlier time period. At those moments, we become aware of 'being' a child of the twenties, a youth of the sixties.

Such moments do not usually last very long. It is as though the waters of ordinary living close up again very swiftly over these briefly emerging vistas. As Christopher Priest writes, we do not as a rule notice the signs of time passing on our own faces, or those of intimates and friends – we learn, in fact, somehow to disregard them.

He was just as I remembered him, but this was impossible. We were both fifteen years older, and he must have been in his late forties when I last saw him. His hair was grey, and thin on the crown; his neck and eyes were heavily wrinkled; there was a stiffness in his right arm, which he remarked on once or twice. He could not possibly have looked like this before, yet sitting there in the hotel restaurant with him I was reassured by the familiarity of his appearance.

I thought of other people I had met again after a period of time. There was always the first surprise, an internal jolt: he has changed, she looks older. Then, within a few seconds, the perception changes and all that can be seen are the similarities. The mind adjusts, the eye allows; the ageing process, the differences of clothes and hair and possessions are edited out by the will to detect continuity. Memory is mistrusted in the recognition of more important identifications. Body-weight might differ, but a person's height or bone-structure do not. Soon it is as if nothing at all has altered. The mind erases backwards, re-creating what one remembers.*

People differ, however, in the extent to which they consciously mark the passage of time in their own lives. There are some people for whom personal records – school reports, family albums, letters, diaries, certificates – document their progress through time, and, in doing this, represent in some sense the meaning of that progress. For others, who experience their lives differently, this kind of record may seem trivial or irrelevant.

However, it is probably rather seldom that the number of years we have lived represents the central theme in our experience of ourselves. For many people, in fact, their chronological age seems sometimes not merely irrelevant, but actually wrong. The man appointed headteacher in the school he attended as a pupil, who feels himself to be the cheekiest of imposters as he sits down in the headmaster's chair – surely that man echoes the feelings many people continue to experience throughout their lives. The sense which Cyril Connolly describes, in *Enemies of Promise*, of being, like a child, permanently under the invisible scrutiny and judgment of those in positions of unassailable authority, seems to be quite a common experience.

I was now entering the third hot room of English education; from St Wulfric's I had got a scholarship to Eton, from Eton to Balliol and from thence there would, I supposed, be other scholarships awaiting me. I could not imagine a moment when I should not be receiving marks for something, when 'poor' or 'very fair' or 'Beta plus' was not being scrawled across my conduct-sheet by the Great Examiner . . . In fact were I to deduce any system from my feelings on leaving Eton, it might be called *The Theory of Permanent Adolescence*. It is the theory that the experiences undergone by boys at the great public schools, their

* Priest, C., *The Affirmation*, Faber, 1981.

glories and disappointments, are so intense as to dominate
their lives and to arrest their development.*

There is a saying that you are as young as you feel. Is this
merely wishful thinking, or does it say what is profoundly true? If
chronological time, in the form of age, seems an unsatisfactory
way of defining a person, perhaps this is because time itself, in
the way we experience it, is not regular. At one level, this means
that some periods of life can be very long, while others pass in
a flash. People often seem to experience childhood, both as
children and in retrospect, as encompassing an almost limitless
stretch of time, of huge tediums or endless summers. As one gets
older, life often speeds up, bringing a sense of incredulity at the
accelerated passing of the years, or the absolute transformations
of younger people. It is as though time had a differential length, a
differential speed, relating to one's own position in the human
life cycle.

Yet even this way of defining time – and, by implication, age –
does not seem to be adequate. A person is, ultimately, not any *one*
age. We all carry with us, encompass within ourselves, something of the people we have been. It is to these people, intimately
familiar, though partly 'other', that we constantly turn. Such
recourse to our earlier selves is not just a matter of conscious
recollection of our childhoods. Intuitively, we draw upon such
aspects of ourselves in our dealings with younger people; we
'know' something of what life must mean to a child because we
still have at least partial access to the child we ourselves once
were.

Nor is it only our past lives that, as human beings, we
encompass. We are also, in some sense, the people we will
become. Perhaps especially through our family engagements, we
come to understand something of the meaning of our future lives.
The intimacy of that context means that even quite young
children have some share in the kinds of events which they may
later encounter. A father who is laid off, a brother who gets

* Connolly, C., *Enemies of Promise*, Routledge & Kegan Paul, 1938.

married, a sister who starts at secondary school – these things, with all their personal ramifications, become part of the stuff of a young child's life. Such a child is not just a spectator, but in a sense actually participates in these personal events. And of course children are constantly encouraged, both explicitly and implicitly, to live in the future. It is not only a matter of the familiar question, 'And what do you want to be when you grow up?' The perspective from which adults habitually view the behaviour of children is itself future-oriented. What a child does is usually valued, passed over or taken as cause for anxiety, because of what it implies for the child's future development – how he or she is likely to turn out later.

What all this can mean for children themselves is vividly illustrated in a recent book by Carolyn Steedman, *The Tidy House*.* The subject of this book is a story written jointly by three nine-year-old girls in a school writing project – a story which they called *The Tidy House*. As the author shows, these three little girls do not merely forecast and describe their own probable future lives; they actually speak, in their story, as the working-class mothers they will become. In their own voice they convey, first hand, all the complicated feelings – the wanting, the resentment, the weariness – of mothers whose inescapable destiny it is to have children who will untidy the tidy house. In this sense, these girls, though only nine years old, *are already* the mothers they will be – the mothers whose lives will replicate those of their own affectionate but hard-pressed and often exasperated mothers.

Our future lives are also, in some sense, present for us as adults. Sometimes, again, this takes the form of what we know through our families. To experience a 'new' event – becoming a parent, being bereaved, moving to a new country – may be to enter into something which was already partly ours, because it had happened to a person we were close to. If we look forward to the next phase of our lives or a phase more distant than that, and try to envisage what it may entail, this is not venturing into entirely strange territory, but dwelling on what we already partly

* Steedman, C., *The Tidy House*, Virago, 1982.

possess – through our intimate experience of others who have entered or passed through these phases.

If we think of individuals as encompassing, at any period in their lives, something of both their past and their future, it becomes evident that some people have much easier and fuller access to their past and future selves than do others. If you ask anyone about their lives as children, this is very clear. Some people can describe, with the richest and most vivid of details, what it was like at five, on the first day at school, or how, at seven, the birth of a younger sister altered life for ever. Other people meet such inquiries with puzzled blankness; they can remember nothing at all before the age of twelve, and have little to say about their teenage lives either. It is as though, for such people, there exists a chasm between their young selves, and the person they now feel themselves to be. A similar difference emerges with respect to the period of old age. There are many people who anticipate life as an old person only with the greatest reluctance, and who seem to operate a vital internal disjunction between themselves and those who are now old. Few people, perhaps, are *not* like this. Yet, as Browning's Rabbi ben Ezra suggests, happy anticipations of old age are possible:

Grow old along with me
The best is yet to be
The last of life for which the first was made.

Fundamental in all this must be the attitude we take towards the different phases of human life. On one level, it is difficult to recall or anticipate periods which do not seem even remotely consonant with one's life in the present. And in general, people feel most comfortable in dwelling, psychologically, in the periods of life which relate most closely to what they value. It is easier to relive, or to anticipate, times in which life seemed, or seems likely, to offer possibilities for positive experience, than to immerse oneself in times where opportunities are shut off, and one's own role is ignominious.

In our society, there is probably a very high level of

agreement as to the positive or negative quality of the different life phases. One way of thinking about this is to consider how people react to the comment, 'How you've changed!' For children and adolescents, this remark is usually very gratifying – a sign that one is leaving childhood behind, and moving on towards adulthood, when real life can begin. Yet how differently the comment is received later on. Women, in particular, feel it to convey a keenly wounding judgement – a statement of their failure to stay young, the failure to disguise their progress towards middle and old age.

It is perhaps our relations with our past and future selves that govern how we stand towards those who are older or younger than we are. For those people to whom their own childhood remains a closed book – an unknown, alien place in which they cannot find anything of the person they now are – for such people, children and their childishness may be not merely mysterious, but embarrassing, even threatening. Elderly people must constitute a similar kind of threat to those who cannot allow themselves to envisage their own potentialities for being old. Conversely, when people feel a special sympathy, a particular resonance, with any one age group, this must arise out of their sense of the richness, the meaningfulness of that phase in their own lives. It is people who – whatever their age – can still dwell in their own adolescence, that are most likely to feel a sense of genuine rapport with modern teenagers.

In so far as old age, and, to a lesser extent, childhood, are experienced negatively by many people in our society, this must mean that there is often an unwillingness to step personally into the shoes of the elderly or of the young. It is then both easier, and psychologically more comfortable, to exclude members of these age groups from full participation in ordinary life – so that one does not have constantly to contemplate their existence. This exclusion in turn reinforces our sense of the old and the young as not entirely fit to contribute to ordinary life, as being different from ourselves in vitally important ways.

It is a truism that our attitudes towards the young and the old, and the ways we deal with them in our society, are not like those of other human societies that are known about. Social anthropologists have described the full participation of children in the economic and social life of some non-Western societies, and the special respect and value accorded in others to the very old. Social historians, documenting our own society in earlier times, have shown how children's lives were continuous with those of adults in pre-industrial society, and that even the *concept* of childhood, as a special, different state, is of quite recent origin. As for elderly people, the extended family of earlier centuries entailed a significant and valued contribution on their part to the domestic economy and the everyday life of the household.

Given that our own practices and attitudes towards childhood and old age are not the only ones possible, it seems important to stand back and consider them critically. Probably the most obvious feature of the social situation of children and old people is their relegation to institutions simply on the basis of their chronological age. Full-time attendance at school is compulsory for people of fifteen downwards. For the elderly, confinement in a special old people's institution is much less widespread – it occurs, in fact, for only a minority of people over sixty-five. But the mere existence of such institutions – set up not to cater for any special need or difficulty but merely to contain the old, as old people – speaks of the assumption that old age justifies exclusion from ordinary life. Old and young people are also alike in being barred from full-time paid work: via compulsory retirement and compulsory school attendance.

Exclusion from work means exclusion from many things – a structure for living in, a recognizable social identity, companionship and solidarity with other workers. It also means economic deprivation, in a society which places a high value on material possessions, and defines the worth of individuals in terms of their earning capacity. To be economically deprived is not just to be without the desirable consumer goods that most people expect to have. Nor is it only to be unable to achieve economic independence – to set up a household of one's own, to make one's own life without the constraints and the anxiety of financial dependence. Finally, economic deprivation can mean, in some sense, experiencing a diminution of oneself as a person, and carry, potentially, a sense of shame and inadequacy.

If we look at things in this way, the treatment of people according to their age begins to assume a political dimension of meaning. In our society, the politics of age render some life phases more rewarding, more powerful, more prestigious, than others. From this point of view, the contempt – however kindly – that is generally accorded to the old and the young, can be seen as a product, not of their personal limitations, but of society's oppression. This, of course, is not the view we generally take. Nor is it the usual perspective of children and the elderly themselves. Yet the impact of the Children's Rights movement, on the one hand, and the Grey Panthers movement on the other – effecting a sense of personal liberation in those who have become involved in them – suggests the meaningfulness of this way of seeing things.

From this standpoint, our experience of time and age is governed by the way we regulate things in our society. There are, though, aspects of that experience which seem to transcend particular social attitudes and social organizations. Our pre-occupation with time, our sense that time is somehow mysterious – ultimately this may have to do with the fact that psychological time is not chronological time. As human beings, we seem to encompass within ourselves our pasts and our futures as well as our presents. Through our engagements in the lives of others, our sense of continuity with past and future history, we transcend, in some sense, the limits of our own physical existence. Ultimately, time, as we experience it in human life, does not itself seem linear – its progression is not straightforward.

One way of realizing this is to reflect on the common assumption that time brings experience and therefore wisdom. If this were the simple truth, how very different human history would be. If people could profit from the mistakes, the suffering, the cruelties of earlier civilizations, then each successive society could step further and further towards human justice, tolerance, compassion. As time progressed, human life would become perceptibly wiser, better. Yet can it really be said that civilization progresses as time proceeds, or that our own society represents a significant advance over that of ancient China?

The non-additiveness of what is brought by time can also be experienced in the relations of older and younger generations. How many parents try to teach their children the lessons they have learned – to save those children the bitter experience through which they themselves bought their wisdom! And yet it seems that no one can build directly upon the experience of another person. Somehow the next generation has to travel its own journey, and perhaps lose its way, without benefit of the accumulated experience of those who have taken their journeys further:

She bade me take love easy, as the grass grows on the weirs,
But I was young and foolish, and now am full of tears.

It is even true that the passing of the years does not necessarily bring gifts of understanding within one's own life. Twenty years' experience, it has been said, may be no more than one year's experience repeated twenty times. And it is possible, too, actually to forget the lessons one has learned through living – to find oneself discovering again what previously seemed crucial and unforgettable. In this sense, time does not bring an accumulation of experience.

These aspects of time, and how we experience it, seem to underlie the complicated meaning of judgments about people in relation to their chronological age. On one level, we expect people to 'be their age'; it is not a compliment to be called immature – nor, conversely, to be called precocious. But there is more to it than that. Though childishness and naivety are generally frowned on, to be childlike, to have retained one's innocence, and sense of wonder, is to be seen as possessing rare qualities that are all too often lost as time goes on.

All these matters relate to the understanding which, as human beings, we have of time and its passage. A central component of this understanding is our developmental psychology – that is, the way we believe the passing of time affects human beings as they progress from birth to death. It is appropriate, therefore, to go on to consider our understanding of the three phases into which most people would divide the life-span.

3 YOUNG LIFE

In our ordinary psychology, as well as within official psychology, we think of youth as occupying a distinctive position in the human life-span, as having a character which is qualitatively different from that of adulthood or old age. And this character is something which most people feel they understand. In psychology, many more textbooks have been written about children and adolescents that about older people. But one does not have to be a psychologist to feel entitled to make pronouncements on the condition of childhood. Nearly everyone – regardless of whether they are parents or teachers or have much personal experience of young people – is prepared to express an opinion, to make judgments, for instance, about the failings of the modern young and about what should be done to put them right. Few people who make such pronouncements would be prepared to express similarly global generalizations about adults. It is the view we hold of the nature of young people, because they are young, that allows most of us to feel such confidence in our judgments.

Central to the way we view children, and the way we regulate their lives, is the assumption that, because they are still young, they do not as yet know much. That is why they must go to school. When we think of what children are like right at the beginning of their school lives, this assumption does often seem to be borne out. All but a few children, on their first day at school, seem very helpless, foolish, inept. It seems they have everything to learn. Let us look at one example of this, in the account which Laurie Lee has given of his first school day.

> I spent that first day picking holes in paper, then went home in a smouldering temper.

'What's the matter, Love? Didn't he like it at school, then?'

'They never gave me the present.'

'Present? What present?'

'They said they'd give me a present.'

'Well now, I'm sure they didn't.'

'They did! They said, "You're Laurie Lee, aren't you? Well, just you sit there for the present." I sat there all day but I never got it. I ain't going back there again.'*

Laurie Lee's experience is probably typical of that of many children when they first go to school. Most children look – and feel – ignorant when they enter the school gates. Yet even five-year-olds are really far from ignorant. By the time they start school, all children possess rich resources of human understanding. If only through tagging along with Mum in her daily routine, young children have learned much about the way people live, the way people relate to each other, the way matters are organized. What kinds of thing happen in buses, shops, post office, clinic – what transactions are done, how people behave, what is possible and not possible – all this is familiar territory. The domestic scene, the domain of women with young children, is, of course, intimately known by five-year-olds, most of whom will, too, have visited homes other than their own. Many children have, by this age, acquired a specialized knowledge of their own. The experiences of play school, nursery groups or being 'minded', bring their own insider's understandings, as does that of being taken into care, or living with parents who are breaking up. A few children, through the circumstances of their family housing, spend much of their pre-school lives outside the house and become 'street-wise'. Others have, by the time they start school, become aware of the meaning of their own ethnic minority status – they know already how to be inconspicuous in public, what places to avoid and what kinds of trouble they and their families may meet. And children of five have not acquired all these kinds

* Lee, L., *Cider with Rosie*, Hogarth Press, 1963.

of understanding by being merely spectators on life; in one way or another, they are already active participants in living.

Despite all this, we think of childhood as essentially entailing incompetence. Children's lack of competence forms the constant basic theme of psychological research, which typically focuses on what a child *cannot* do, rather than on what he or she can. More generally, we view the young in the perspective of helplessness, ignorance, neediness – as requiring to be guided, taught, brought up. The whole institution of schooling, which so distinctively marks off the situation of young people from that of their elders, is, of course, based on this perspective. It is being at school that essentially defines the condition of childhood in our society. Having to go to school until you are sixteen means being subject to a legal compulsion arising simply out of being young. The sphere of compulsion is itself massive; as the title of a recent book puts it, school life stretches over fifteen thousand hours.*

A major aspect of the institution of school is that it separates the lives of children and adolescents from the lives of older people. It means that the young spend the major part of their waking hours in contexts that are different from those in which adults are living. As a result, schools represent a major disjunction between the lives of adults and children – a disjunction in day-to-day experience, in social relationships and in status. This cuts both ways. It is not just that children are barred from access to or participation in many of the vital spheres of ordinary adult life. On their side, adults remain cut off, excluded, from the world of school. For all but a very few men and women, school represents essentially unknown, mysterious territory. Particularly to those whose own experience as a school pupil was difficult, unhappy or unsuccessful, schools may seem not merely foreign, but alienating, intimidating places. When their own children's schooling is at issue, probably few parents actually manage to traverse this huge divide. Quite early on, the question 'What did you do at school today?' seems to get a dusty answer. Communication, on both sides, is achieved with difficulty; it is

* Rutter, M., *et al.*, *Fifteen Thousand Hours*, Open Books, 1979.

hard to speak about a world with which the other person is so unfamiliar.

Essentially, school is set up to be an institution of learning. To most people it would probably seem obvious that, in school, children do learn; most basically, they learn how to read, write and count, and this is followed by the acquisition of a broad spectrum of information about the world they live in – science, history, the arts, technical crafts, foreign languages and so on. How this learning takes place does not seem a particularly complicated matter. Children sit in classrooms, for lessons, with teachers who are experts on what they teach and, in addition, have been trained how to impart their knowledge to children.

The kinds of thing that children are expected to learn at school sometimes include an understanding of simple economic principles, such as those of profit and loss. This sort of understanding was a focus of a study which was carried out recently by a British psychologist, Gustav Jahoda.* Jahoda wanted to see whether elementary principles of profit and loss were understood better by British nine-year-old children, or by nine-year-olds in the Zimbabwe township of Harare. Whereas in Britain very few children have direct personal experience of buying and reselling at a profit, children in Harare often participate directly in their parents' small trading. In order to see how well the two groups of children understood simple economics, Jahoda set up a mock shop situation, and played a shopping game with each child during which he asked the child a number of questions about prices, profit margins and so on. From the way the children responded, it was clear that British and Harare nine-year-olds had very different levels of understanding. Most English and Scottish nine-year-olds were very much at sea when trying to explain how a shop actually functions. For instance, most of them thought that shopkeepers buy goods for the same price as they sell them. Even children who realized that selling prices are higher than buying ones, thought that shopkeepers would put any money they made

* Jahoda, G. (1983), European 'lag' in the development of an economic concept: a study in Zimbabwe, *British Journal of Development Psychology*, *I*, 113–20.

to purely personal use. By contrast, most nine-year-olds in Harare had not only mastered the concept of profit; they also understood that part of earnings had to be put aside to buy other goods.

It seems from Jahoda's investigation that, despite their more sophisticated level of schooling, British children understand much less than do these African children about the financial transactions of shopping and trading that take place in both their worlds. The difference is clearly due to the personal familiarity, the direct personal involvement, of the African children in the transactions at issue. Through their own engagements in their parents' small trading, rather than from any formal teaching on the part of their parents, the Harare children had picked up, absorbed, understood the underlying principles of trading. Evidently children are able to learn what they have not been explicitly taught – to assimilate, through a kind of osmosis, what is happening around them, if they can directly participate in it.

This way of seeing children is not easily squared with the view that the young need to be taught, guided, brought to understanding by adults. It carries, too, some implicit questions about schooling. Though children do undoubtedly learn at school, perhaps they acquire their most significant understandings, not so much through being formally taught, as from what they pick up through their own engagements. If this is so, we have to ask about all the ways in which children personally involve themselves in their school lives, and how they position themselves in relation to others in their school contexts. Because we assume that learning means being taught, it is to teachers and teaching that we habitually look as the significant factors in schooling. In considering teachers, we think about their knowledge, their skills, their expertise as teachers – yet it may be the *person* of a teacher, and how as another *person*, a particular pupil stands towards her, which is ultimately far more crucial.

But perhaps, even then, teachers themselves are less significant in children's engagements than are other children. Although pupils' inter-relationships are generally passed over entirely in the organizing of class groups – age being seen as the only relevant common denominator – the composition of a new class is usually of the utmost concern to children themselves. Whether a particular intimate friend, an ally, the group of one's own mates will be there – whether the class will contain sworn enemies, or last year's playground bully, whether one will be isolated in an unfamiliar or hostile group – for most children these are hardly incidental matters, but personally urgent questions. Nor are classrooms the only setting where significant personal negotiations take place between children; momentous encounters can occur in the playground, the corridors, outside the school gates.

If we were to define these essentially social aspects as constituting the raw material from which children learn at school, what kind of learning would this entail? Here is a young woman describing her experience in science lessons, as a secondary school pupil:

> Science was to me an opportunity to be feminine. That meant posing around the experiments, instead of taking part. It meant watching for the teacher's response and not watching the outcome of the experiment. It meant being foolish; making a big fuss when there was flame, bangs and so on from the things we were doing. It meant asking the boys or the teacher for help – gazing into their eyes and asking them to explain . . . It wasn't my parents any more to whom I went for the presents and the pat on the back. It was the males around me . . . What did get me approval was being vague and dumb, letting them help me with my work, seeking their guidance.*

Like most secondary schoolgirls, this pupil had learned, through her school experience, how to conduct herself in her lessons in a suitably 'feminine' way. Such learning would hardly have been taught by her science teacher; on the contrary, he would certainly have been dismayed to realize that his teaching had been 'read' in this way by his girl pupils. Nor would pupils have explicitly taught each other to behave like this – even were

* Brewster, E., 'Schooldays, schooldays', chapter in Spender and Sarah (eds.), *Learning to Lose*, Writers and Readers, 1982.

they able to spell out all the complex and subtle aspects of being 'feminine'.

Gender constitutes one of the most fundamental ways of relating to other human beings; it is a basic kind of position vis-à-vis others. Though gender is not on the school timetable, nor taught by the teachers in schools, children seem to learn it for themselves, through their inter-relationships with teachers and with other pupils. This is not the only position towards others that unofficial school learning can offer. Children also come to learn, through their school experience, what it means, for themselves personally, to belong to an ethnic minority.

This is Doreen, an eleven-year-old London girl, talking to Thomas Cottle:

> You're walking down the corridor, and a boy calls you a coloured pig, or golliwog. . . . So I tell my mother about it and she calls the school and talks to this person or that person, and they keep telling her the same thing, like, we'll try to stop it, how can we watch out for all the children all the time, are you sure Doreen isn't doing anything to start it? You almost have to get hit like I did before they believe it goes on even when people are just minding their own business.
>
> But every time there's trouble, and there is a lot of the time, my mother or father will say, 'Well, let's hope it won't happen again. Maybe this is the last of it.' They know this isn't the last of it. But what can they do?*

As this kind of testimony shows, children are often perfectly conscious of political aspects of their existence. Nor does this apply only to ethnic minorities. Schools themselves are, of course, hierarchical; in school, boys and girls come to be graded in terms of academic success and failure. When I sat in on a number of school classrooms a few years ago, it was very clear that by the age of twelve, at least, most children had a definite

* Cottle, T. J., *Black Testimony: Voices of Britain's West Indians*, Wildwood House, 1978.

awareness of where they and others stood in the academic status hierarchy. Often this meant distancing themselves from the 'snobs', the 'posh people', the 'brain-boxes' in the class.

It seems that for most children, their relationships with other people are very important. It seems, too, that, while still far from adulthood, boys and girls have come to understand very well the way in which dimensions of gender, race or status in the hierarchy affect such relationships in our society. This understanding is not just academic, for children themselves actually *operate* socially in terms of these dimensions. All this surely involves a paradox. Children are sent to school because, as yet, they are unready to enter the world of adults; they do not understand how that adult world is constituted and regulated. Yet, in school, they seem to be living lives that are closely similar to those of adults – lives in which just the same kinds of human concerns are involved and just the same kinds of factors are salient within those concerns.

It is, of course, our sense that children are essentially different, other, that underlies the way we regulate their lives. This sense is central to the official psychology of childhood. One aspect is that children are portrayed as basically incompetent, as lacking the kinds of understanding upon which adults base their lives. Another aspect is the depiction of the young as not really responsible for their lives, not really agents in their own right, because they are seen as subjects, recipients, of influences and guidance from others. Neither of these two views seems to square with a close examination of the lives of most children. Attending closely to how children themselves experience their lives also calls into question the generality with which psychology – and conventional wisdom – endows them. Like adults, boys and girls are very singular, particular human beings.

This particularity tends to emerge clearly in the voices of individual children. I should like to take as an example an autobiography written by a sixteen-year-old boy, Sabir Bandali. In this story, Sabir describes his childhood in Uganda, growing up in his Indian family, until, when he was twelve, the family were forced to flee to England from the violence and terror of Idi

Amin. In order to set these events in a wider perspective, he prefaces the story of his own cross-continental journey to London with a detailed and vivid account of his father's journey, at the age of sixteen, from India to East Africa. Sabir then resumes the story of his own early experience at home and school in South London, and of his father's sudden death. Here are some extracts from the concluding passages of this autobiography:

> Up to my father's death, I was an ordinary young boy. I had been born into poverty and had grown up at an ordinary pace. I had believed or taken for granted many things, and had obeyed my elders (especially my father) even when I didn't want to . . . After my father's death, I had to grow up at an extraordinary pace. I was no longer a young boy, but a young man, especially at home where I was the eldest male . . . It's eight o'clock on a typical November evening . . . and here I am, sitting at a table, thinking and scribbling down memories, wondering whether I'll ever be able to remember my past, when I was a young kid of nine being entered into public school for the first time – the days when I didn't have too much to worry about . . . Something's missing. The world is a world short; the house is full, and yet it's empty. It will never be completely full again.
>
> 'What will you do when you grow up, Sabir?'
> I remember my father testing me. . . .
> 'Will you get married and leave me? Will you forget I fathered you? You will say "My father is old and useless now. There is no need to stay with him." You will disown me. Isn't that true?'
> His words were cruel, but moving . . .
> And now? Now he's gone, and I can't even show him how much of a son of his I am. I pick up a cigarette and light it. I hold back the tears and inhale the comforting smoke.*

* Bandali, S., 'Small accidents', chapter in *Our Lives*, I.L.E.A. English Centre, 1979.

Sabir entitles this autobiography 'Small Accidents'. His life is, of course, very unlike the lives of most children who grow up in our society. Few children have been uprooted from one country and forced to flee to another. Most children have fathers who are still alive. It is rare, while still young, to have to take on adult responsibilities in the family. Yet perhaps Sabir's 'small accidents' – atypical and traumatic as they are – merely represent extreme versions of the very particular incidents, the personally significant events, which make up the vital experience of every child's life. Certainly children themselves, when asked about their lives, typically tell very personal stories – stories which are far from standardized, stories of unique protagonists each on their own unique journey.

We tend to define children by the age they are, to think of a particular young person as being *at* the chronological age they happen to have reached at that moment. But in his own story, Sabir's relation to time does not seem so simple. Somehow in himself, Sabir encompasses his father's time too – a momentous period in his father's young life which he is able to re-create and, as it were, live through himself. Sabir's own early years, and their poignant contrast with his life now, are also vividly alive to him. And, more fundamentally, in the lonely heart-searching out of which he comes to write his story, Sabir reflects on what has happened in his life and what it all means. That two-year-old conversation, recaptured word for word, is mulled over, deeply and with pain. Not fully understood at the time, his father's words now take on a new and profoundly important meaning – a meaning to which Sabir can now never respond, which he can never show his father he has understood.

Young people, like older people, have their pasts. For Sabir, this past means irrevocable loss: 'Something's missing. The world is a world short.' In this, as in other fundamental components of human experience, perhaps the young are no different from the rest of us – we who, as adults, are apt so often to look back with wonder and longing to our earlier lives.

If we make a global comparison between younger and older people, it is probably broadly true that most children are less knowledgeable and less competent than most adults. But this seems to be largely a function of their lack of *experience* in the world of human affairs, rather than of any lack of basic *capacity*. While there may be very good reasons for segregating the young from some of the routines of adult life – in particular, to protect them from exploitation – we should not confuse their consequent ignorance and incompetence with any fundamental deficiency within them. Though their situation may be different, children do seem, *as persons*, to be very like their elders.

4 BEING OLD

Once, when I was six, I asked a much loved and intimately known elderly companion a question I often thought about myself. It was what she would wish for, in all the world, if she could have one wish. I was familiar with stories in which people were granted their dearest wish, and they were stories in which I loved to place myself, and imagine that I could marry the beautiful prince, possess the white charger with the gold and scarlet trappings, or live for ever in the magic kingdom beneath the lake. But my elderly friend referred to none of these things. She thought about the question for a little while and then said, 'I should wish for good health.' This answer, I remember, surprised me very much. It was not merely that my friend did not seem to care about the kinds of imaginary treasures I liked so much to dwell on. It was also that it was barely possible to understand what she did refer to, since the idea of *health* did not, for me, have any real meaning. Looking back, I think this incident must have produced a momentary revelation of the very different subjective worlds that people can inhabit.

If health plays little part in the preoccupations of the young, there are many reasons why it should be central to those of the old. It is, of course, perfectly obvious that physical ageing entails physical losses and physical vulnerabilities. Increased proneness to illness, disease and injury, reduced stamina, a slowing of recuperative powers – all these are conditions which old people necessarily have to face. However, the degree of disability consequent upon these physical changes varies a great deal among

Part of this chapter was originally published by the Beth Johnson Foundation in their booklet, *Liberation of the Elders*. The Foundation's permission for its publication here is gratefully acknowledged.

different individuals. Often this is the decisive factor governing the kind of life which an old person is allowed to live.

As things are now, most old people in our society probably live somewhere between two sorts of existence. It is likely to be their health, as well as their family and housing situation, and their economic resources which are critical in determining which of the two they experience. When these things are favourable, the old are generally able to maintain a way of life in which they possess a reasonable degree of autonomy. But unless they are unusually lucky, participation in the main areas of human life will have been drastically curtailed. An old person no longer holds that passport to social recognition and social respect – a job. In family life, they are likely to be denied a responsible role in a household in which the young grow up. Together with this deprivation of such significant adult parts in life, probably goes at least some measure of social isolation and personal loneliness. The guaranteed daily contacts of work and family have been lost; and relative immobility, impoverishment, and isolated accommodation may make it hard for elderly people to organize such contacts for themselves.

Such a life is unlikely to be particularly happy; but it cannot be compared with the misery of those living another sort of existence. This is the life of old people who have been consigned to institutions. Such places range from old people's homes to geriatric wards in general or psychiatric hospitals. In all these contexts, a common denominator is the loss of personal identity, personal autonomy, which even the most humanely run institutions are bound to entail. The grouping of people together by old age and infirmity, the loss of one's own surroundings and possessions, the submission to an impersonal and unchosen routine of living, and frequently, the involuntary nature of one's presence there – all these things stand in bitter contrast to the freedom and respect to which most adults have been accustomed. For those unlucky enough to suffer serious infirmity, or disability, the attending to intimate bodily and personal needs by successive shifts of staff, who, however skilled, do not know one as an individual, may add a further sense of demoralization. For most people living out the years in such contexts, their experience is likely to be one of being diminished as a human being.

As with childhood, age is paramount in the way we, in our society, view late life and, concomitantly, in how we arrange it. And central to the meaning with which we invest age, at this life phase, is the idea of incompetence. This is what underlies the allocation of many old people to one sort of institution or another. Housing the elderly like this is seen as an inevitable consequence of their physical incompetence. It is assumed that old people, even if they are not actually bedridden, are unable to manage on their own because of their physical frailty. The logical thing to do, therefore, is to place them in settings designed to provide physical care and supervision. So putting an old person into an old people's home is seen as responding appropriately to his or her current physical needs.

Though it is perfectly true that the old are weaker, more fragile, less alert, more prone to illness and generally less physically competent than younger adults – though all this is true, perhaps such a comparison is itself essentially irrelevant. All that may matter is the relationship between a person's physical powers, and the physical demands of the situation they live in. If an old woman's bodily resources are *adequate* to cope with her context, perhaps that is what counts. And frequently elderly people, aware of their limitations and liabilities, have established a physical setting and a routine which conserves their energies and minimizes risks. Where some aspects of living in a familiar setting become too difficult for someone living alone, there is often the regular or occasional help of a neighbour, or someone in the family. Such a solution certainly seems physically sounder than total removal to an institution, where strength and vitality may quickly fail in the wake of drastic personal uprooting.

Fundamentally, the institutionalization of old people seems to ignore the irrelevance of judgments about physical competence without reference to physical demands. No one would dream of supposing that a child had entered a physical decline because he could no longer put his toes into his mouth, as he could in babyhood. That is not a skill that the circumstances of childhood demand of him. In the same way, it makes nonsense to pronounce an old woman to be totally dependent on physical support, just because it now takes her longer to climb her stairs than it used to, and she needs to lie down from time to time during the day. If that is her life, and she can cope with it, perhaps it is her competence rather than her incompetence which should be acknowledged.

Because old people are viewed from a perspective which emphasizes their incompetence, the idea of their *dependence* is a crucial one. It is important to consider what is implied by defining the old as essentially dependent people. One aspect of this definition is its separation of 'the elderly' from 'adults', who are conventionally seen as *not* dependent – although, as we shall see later, this assumption does not seem a sound one. But by defining the old as dependent, we apparently make them comparable with children who, similarly, are subject to special institutional arrangements set up to cater for their dependency needs. And yet our view of their two kinds of dependencies is not quite the same.

Imagine a toddler living at home among his family. Just like somebody very old, he needs a lot of physical support in managing life. He must be helped with parts of his dressing and undressing. He is not up to using a knife properly, and some of his food may need cutting up for him. He may be incontinent occasionally, when he will need help in being cleaned and changed. He may have to have a helping hand coming downstairs; and on long walks he may get so tired that he will have to be put in his pushchair. And so on. All these are demands made by the physically weak and incompetent upon those around them. Yet think of the different significance we give these supporting activities, according to whether they are done for a young child or an old person. Essentially, physical support is given gladly to the young, grudgingly to the old. This has to do, it seems, with the fact that the old have a long past, while the young have a long future. The question of why the future should be accorded so much more value than the past, is something we shall need to come back to later in this chapter.

Like so many other aspects of our view of life in relation to time, the view of old age as a time of incompetence is given apparent scientific validity by the pronouncements of psychology. It is their focus on deficiency which is the most noticeable feature of psychological texts which cover the period of late human life. The major part of such accounts is usually devoted to a retailing of intellectual deficits. After a description of the neurological damage wrought in the cerebral cortex by the passage of time, the supposed consequences in mental functioning are presented. Memory loss, the incapacity to absorb new material, perseveration and rigidity are described, and documented by reference to laboratory studies where old people have been formally tested and their performance compared with that of younger people. Usually such features are summarized by the statement that intelligence falls off dramatically in old age, with a large vocabulary being the only residue of the person's previous repertoire of abilities. Having thus demolished the possibility of any intellectual assets in the elderly, texts like these turn, usually more briefly, to the emotional side. Here again, deterioration is the theme. The old person is presented as having regressed to an earlier, more primitive personal adjustment, with an egocentric outlook and a lack of mature emotional control.

Leaving aside the artificiality of much of the research which is the basis of this kind of account, and assuming, for the sake of argument, that these features *are* characteristic of many old people, we have to ask why this should be so. Though neurological deterioration undoubtedly occurs over time, even severe brain damage does not always conquer the human spirit. There is eloquent testimony to this in a remarkable book written by a neurologist, Oliver Sachs.* The book tells the story of twenty New York survivors of the sleeping-sickness epidemic of the 1920s. Sachs made a very close study of these men and women when, many years after the onset of their illness, they were given a 'miracle' awakening drug, L-DOPA.

The central theme of this unusual book is the capacity of many human beings somehow to face reality and achieve sanity,

* Sachs, O.W., *Awakenings*, Penguin Books, 1976.

while in the midst of bizarre, often terrifying experiences. The story of Mrs Hester Y. serves as an example. As a young woman, Hester was a person of warmth, humour and independence. She had married, had a son and a daughter, and enjoyed ten years of family life when she was struck by illness in her thirtieth year. Her early symptoms took the form of occasional episodes during which she became temporarily motionless and seemingly 'not there'. Gradually the change became more marked, until at thirty-five, she was virtually immobile, speechless and unreachable. Her admission to hospital at this stage was followed by the complete break-up of her family. Her husband divorced her, her son left home and abandoned family contact, while her daughter became psychotic and was herself institutionalized in a local hospital.

In hospital, Hester herself remained imprisoned in her silent, immobile, remote condition for more than twenty years. Then, on the threshold of old age, she was given the drug L-DOPA. Her reaction was dramatic and grotesque. She experienced sudden bouts of extreme but fluctuating emotion – anguish, terror, rage or uncontrollable hilarity. She saw vivid hallucinations, which succeeded each other at dizzying speed. And she was constantly subject to strange involuntary movements – movements in which, for instance, her right arm would be suddenly bent back so that her fingers rested between her shoulder-blades.

Yet, while suffering all these strange and intimate disturbances, Hester finally found her way to a kind of personal equilibrium. Four years after first taking the drug – years in which these peculiar symptoms remained unabated – she had become so used to her condition that she was able to discuss it with others, even sometimes to laugh about it. Though at first she had felt overwhelmed, and often persecuted, by the strangeness and persistence of the symptoms which constantly assailed her, she gradually came to accept them. As Sachs put it, 'she seems to see them simply *as things that are there*, like her nose, or her name, or New York, or the world'. Even more remarkably, Hester achieved over time a certain skill in managing her symptoms, so that she was able sometimes to prevent or circumvent them, or if not, then somehow to utilize them. This gave her a rare insight into her own condition. Sachs comments that through 'her sharp wit and her bizarre illness [she] achieved a knowledge and a control of her nervous system and reactions which not a neurologist anywhere in the world could approach'. Reflecting on the position Hester had finally reached, Sachs adds: 'She is absolutely "together" and will stay together . . . despite the innumerable odds against her . . . [she] has emphatically awoken and returned to reality.'

Hester's personally triumphant story shows that, somehow, some individuals are able to win through despite suffering the most profoundly disabling neurological illnesses. Fortunately, few people are likely to experience, in their old age, anything approaching the severity of Hester's condition. Yet the conventional wisdom has it that age inevitably brings a deterioration of the person. It may be that where this does occur in old people, it is the product of the arrangements made for them, and the expectations which surround them. Although the pressures, and the constraints, of an elderly person's life may not be easy for someone else readily to imagine, there may be a more accessible parallel in the situation of being in hospital. Where the power to take decisions and act on them is removed, where one is obliged to play a passive and submissive role, where one is almost totally dependent on others, where one has little say over what happens, and where, finally, one may easily feel bereft of dignity – in these circumstances, it is difficult to maintain one's normal self. Psychological horizons quickly become narrowed, so that the concrete details of living become supremely important. Physical discomfort looms large, as does eating, so that a normally mature person may easily become petulant and querulous, or even find herself bursting into tears if she is kept waiting for the commode, or if, instead of the eagerly anticipated dinner, a less attractive one is brought. If this kind of personal deterioration can occur in a matter of a few weeks, how much more likely is it to affect someone living for many years in a similar situation, with no prospect of ever regaining their personal domain.

The official psychology which portrays the old in terms of

deficiency and personal deterioration is the psychology written by people who are not themselves old. Like children, elderly people are not given a voice in defining their condition. If they were, this definition would surely be very different. Here is the first part of a poem written by an elderly patient in a geriatric ward in a Dundee hospital – a poem discovered by one of the nurses after her death.

What do you see nurses, what do you see?
Are you thinking when you are looking at me –
A crabbit old woman, not very wise,
Uncertain of habit, with far-away eyes,
Who dribbles her food and makes no reply,
When you say in a loud voice 'I do wish you'd try'.
Who seems not to notice the things that you do,
And forever is losing a stocking or shoe.
Who, unresisting or not, lets you do as you will,
With bathing and feeding, the long day to fill.
Is that what you are thinking, is that what you see?
Then open your eyes, nurse, you are not looking at me.*

It seems that, within the subjective standpoint of old people themselves, their personal being is not encompassed by their chronological age. For this woman, evidently, being defined in such a way made a cruel mockery of her own experience. And it is, perhaps, supremely improbable that a person's age should define her better than anything else about her – that the mere passage of time should tell us all we need to know of her. It might even be said that a standardized, age-governed view is less and less appropriate as people get older. Just as the lines of the face show most clearly in old age what stance a person has habitually adopted towards their experience, so it may be that the person becomes more themselves and less like anyone else, the further they advance through life.

* Anonymous, 'Crabbit Old Woman', *Beacon House News*, Christmas Issue, 1978, Northern Ireland Association for Mental Health.

But prevailing social attitudes to old people are not rooted in
their own subjective experience; on the contrary, the old are
viewed from a perspective which defines them as 'other', and as
'less'. One of the consequences of this is in the character of the
provision which our society makes for old people. The kind of
social functions, activities, entertainments organized for the
elderly in residential institutions, clubs or centres are essentially
prescribed for them by younger people who have in mind their
limits, their incompetence, their loss of maturity. As a result,
what is offered is probably experienced by most recipients as
trivial, tedious or childish; the activities are not such as to invite
real personal engagement, as activities can be that are freely
chosen and organized for oneself.

An example of this experience is described in a recent book
about old people by David Unruh, aptly titled *Invisible Lives*.
Unruh talked to a number of elderly men and women who lived
in Northern California, U.S.A. Among other questions, he asked
them about the kinds of educational and social activities available
to them. A common experience was of being subject, in leisure
centres, retirement communities, or housing clubs, to activities
chosen *for* them by the middle-aged people who organized such
things. Any suggestions on their own part, about the things they
would actually like to do, tended to be ignored or even contemptuously dismissed. As one elderly woman said,

> At one time, many of us got together and decided we
> would like to have someone from the Bay Area to teach
> transcendental meditation, yoga, and other Eastern ideas.
> Well, I mean to tell you, the woman at the senior center in
> charge of these sorts of things didn't like the idea at all.
> She thought it would be foolish to have 'a bunch of old
> people doing things like that'.

Another of Unruh's interviewees described his visit to the
local senior centre:

> Well, my wife and I went over there once when we first

moved to town. We had heard they occasionally had art activities there, and we wanted to see what was going on. . . .

. . . What we saw were a bunch of people sitting around going through magazines and cutting out pictures for collages and that sort of thing. I think a person can maintain their interest in life if they don't learn how to paste things in scrapbooks, do handiwork, or even play scrabble.*

Unruh's book is about the social worlds of old people. He suggests that the positions of people within their social worlds can be seen in terms of a scale, with *strangers* at one end, and *insiders* at the other. Intermediate between these two poles are *tourists* and *regulars*. The role of a stranger is one of relative ignorance about the social context and, concomitantly, of liability to experience disorientation and confusion within it. Relationships with other members of the group are superficial, and there is a general sense of detachment and lack of commitment to the concerns involved. By contrast, insiders stand at the very heart of their social world, and have an intimate understanding of its concerns. Within their worlds, insiders act as teachers for others and carry personal responsibility for the way things function. It is Unruh's argument that, for elderly people, achieving the role of an insider is almost impossible, and even those of regular and tourist are gained only with considerable effort. Most characteristically, it is to the position of stranger, within their social worlds, that old people are relegated.

If society does generally deprive its older members of chances for significant social engagements, this is because the elderly are seen as having no real contribution to make. It is a judgment of which old people themselves tend to be keenly, painfully aware, and which they sometimes echo in dismissing themselves as 'past it' or 'useless'. To consider what is involved in this kind of

* Unruh, D. R., *Invisible Lives: Social Worlds of the Aged* (pp. 154–5 and 156), Sage Publications, 1983.

attitude, we need to return to the question of the relative values which our society accords to the future and to the past.

A few years ago, in a series of Reith lectures, Edmund Leach built up a vehement case that society should be run by the young. His central argument was that, given the accelerating rate of technological change, anyone older than thirty-five would be insufficiently in touch with contemporary ways of doing things to be capable of any sort of social responsibility. The inescapable implication of this argument is that human life is encompassed by the technology of the age. Such a view does, of course, define the past as simply obsolete, while carrying a high valuation of the future. This devaluation of the past necessarily entails disregarding its representatives – the old.

Yet the past – like the future – is irrelevant only if we deny validity to all that is not currently on stage. To ignore the past is surely to impoverish the present, which has little meaning without reference to what went before. At its grandest, the distillation of past human experience constitutes our civilization. And since we live in history, to understand where we come from tells us something about where we stand now and where we may be able to go. Through past history, we can sometimes see both the relativity of social arrangements, and the continuity of human life – what changes, and what does not change. If the remote past, through documents and clues that have survived, can throw new light on contemporary life, the old, with whom direct intercourse is possible, can surely do so in a far more immediate way. Having lived a long time, an old person is a living link between present and past, who spans the generations, who can bring what has gone before to what is now.

The most basic feature of the old is that they cannot be wholly encompassed by the present. Thoreau's description of the non-conformer also fits the old: 'If a man does not keep step with his companions, perhaps it is because he hears a more distant drummer.' Such a person is, of course, in many ways, an awkward customer – it is easier to put them out of the way as not 'with it' any more. But another way of seeing such people is as carrying within themselves something distinctive, something valuable – something which might give a different perspective to the lives of younger people.

To look at things in this way involves seeing an old person as essentially a witness, a witness of what has been. To be a witness means making a particular kind of contribution to the lives of others. It entails two aspects. As a witness, a person must keep alive in themselves the heritage which they have personally experienced. In this, reminiscence is vital. Though old people are often viewed with contempt as living nostalgically in the past, the effort to retain what one has seen, what one has known, is a necessary one. Nor is it easy to sustain memories when there is no one else to remember them. But a witness must also bear witness. And giving to others from one's own heritage of experience surely means more than telling grandchildren stories about the past. Experience itself usually cannot be communicated, or even felt, from cold. It can be called up only through personal encounters in the present with something of the same kind. Sometimes only when she sees her own daughter being a parent is an old woman able to recall, and talk about, her own experience of parenthood. This is why it is the exclusion of old people from the main arenas of human life that removes the possibility of their unique social contribution.

5 ADULTHOOD

To be grown up! To wear the clothes you choose, eat what you
like, stay up as late as ever you want! To have your own friends,
go anywhere you please! Above all, to be free – no more to have
someone always telling you what to do! Situated in childhood,
how longingly the young look forward to the distant prospect of
adulthood. Nor is it only children for whom the adult years
represent so much the best, the most desirable part of human life.
To the old, their adulthood is all too likely to be the focus of
constant wistful recollection. Ah, but you should have seen me
when I was in my prime!

In how we understand and therefore constitute our human
lives, it is the period of adulthood to which we accord much the
greatest power and prestige. Adulthood is the state towards
which we see childhood as climbing, and from which old age is
seen as declining. Typically, we define the adult years in terms of
material progress. The differences that mark off adults from
children, we see as positive, and, in turn, such changes of circumstance as occur within the period of adulthood itself – at least
up to middle age – we view as progressive. In their picture of what
this means, official psychology and general understanding are
quite similar. Psychological writings about adulthood portray it
as the time of *maturity*. Maturity is itself defined in terms of
autonomy and independence. People are seen as mature to the
extent to which they are functioning independently, having control over their own lives, not relying upon others. The crucial
arenas in which such independence is expected are those of work
and family life. In psychological texts, 'vocational maturity'
means choosing and conducting an occupational career to match
one's aptitudes and interests – a career which will offer a life-long

series of challenges, opportunities for ever deeper personal engagements and greater social recognition. When it comes to the sphere of interpersonal relationships, maturity is defined both in personal and in sexual terms. The mature adult is expected to establish an independent family unit, where children will be born and brought up within the context of a stable heterosexual relationship.

All this accords quite closely with the prevailing view in our society of what adult life means, or should mean. In making judgments about adult men and women – in discussing what someone has made of their life, what that life adds up to – it is typically to the indices of work and family life that people refer. And in looking ahead to their own adult lives, planning the course they mean to take, the overwhelming majority of young men and women cite just these things. To get a good job and get on in it, to get married and have children, to have a nice home of your own – these, to nearly every young person in our society, are the goals to strive for during the years of adult life. So eager are many young people to achieve these goals that they cannot bear to wait, but leave home while still at school, only to find themselves quickly destitute, or embark on teenage pregnancies or marriages which may later be bitterly regretted.

To common sense, it is hardly surprising that getting a good job and establishing one's own family represent the basic goals of adult life, and constitute the measure of human maturity. Work and family are, after all, the two main spheres, the basic arenas of action and experience, for most men and women in our society. Yet perhaps both spheres are far more problematic than we generally acknowledge.

In order to consider what the arena of work may mean in most people's lives, we can take as a starting point the reflections of one particular young woman, living in London. Though Junine, in being black, is atypical, nevertheless her experience in entering the world of employment would probably be echoed by many young white people. Gifted musically, she had hoped to train to be a music teacher. But her father, in poor health and able to earn very little, was under the constant threat of losing his job; the family, in which there were five other children, lived in cramped council housing and were chronically hard up. In these circumstances, Junine decided to leave school and enter work at sixteen, despite her mother's encouragement to pursue her dream of being a music teacher. This is how Junine describes her situation:

> I wanted to say, you're right, Mother. I'll stay at it and become a music teacher. But who's kidding who? . . . We're poor people, baby . . . it didn't take no brains to figure out what a person had to do. If you had any sense left in you, you quit school and went to work. You took whatever they gave you, too, or you let them train you to become anything . . .
>
> So I got a couple of job possibilities. Some turned out, some didn't. But I got a job working with a laundry and cleaning company, you know, not so far from where I live. I said to myself, it isn't what I like to do . . . But listen, I got friends who left school, they still don't have nothing, and I got my job, so it could be worse . . .
>
> . . . Old Buzzy, after the first ten minutes, she says to me, Hey Junine, is this all there is? I mean, is this what you've been doing all these months? I said . . . what could *anybody* do in a laundry that no three-year-old couldn't do? . . . I told her . . . I'm in laundry . . . You keep your mouth shut and keep folding up those sheets. . . . If slavery pays me for forty hours a week and an hour off for lunch, then slavery's my business . . . they don't give you no choices in this game.*

Junine herself would certainly have been at a particular disadvantage within a society which discriminates against its black members. Yet her experience in seeking and maintaining work is probably very much like that of most young people in our society. The idealized portrait shows the young adult carefully selecting

* Cottle, T. J., *Black Testimony: Voices of Britain's West Indians*, Wildwood House, 1978.

from a vast array of possibilities the specific career that will
enable the best possible expression of his or her particular talents
and enthusiasms. The career itself is viewed as stretching out all
the way to retirement, with almost limitless opportunities and
prospects of advancement. For most young people in our society,
reality is surely very different; it is the constraints, rather than
the huge possibilities, which are salient in seeking employment.

Another way of thinking about what work means for most
adults is to consider the response people make to the question,
'What do you do?' Supposedly, occupation represents the most
important index of a person's individuality, a feature which,
more than any other, defines the kind of person they are. Yet
there seem to be very many people to whom this inquiry is uncon-
genial, unwelcome. For all those for whom the nature of their
actual employment was a matter of chance and luck rather than
personal choice from a range of possibilities, the implications
must be inappropriate, even insulting. And to assume that the
work itself is chosen because it is personally fulfilling is to ignore
the fact that, often, the jobs people do entail a daily routine of
drudgery. This is sometimes true of salaried, as well as blue-
collar occupations. And even where their work offers variety,
stimulation or responsibility, still people often feel personally
alienated from it. But the question 'What do you do?' is even
more offensive to those who are not in paid employment at all, for
whom it probably represents one more expression of the reproach
which our society directs at the 'workshy' or 'scroungers'. The
question is also particularly loathed by women, whose household
or family care is not defined or paid as work; the guilty and
resentful answer is usually 'Nothing – I'm only a housewife.'

To ask what people do is often a disguised inquiry about what
they are worth, economically. This must be a powerful dimension in the way most adults experience their occupational lives.
Though for many people who do routine, boring or exhausting
jobs, there are the social satisfactions of companionship, mutual
support, perhaps even shared hardship, earning a reasonable
wage surely plays a major part in making the job worth while.
Ours is a society in which the social status, the general respect,

accorded to adults is to a large extent a function of their material wealth. To have the things that people are expected to have – this is a basic goal in most adults' lives. And even those who are objectively well paid may, subjectively, feel inadequate by comparison with others, who have gained greater promotion, or who work in more highly paid professions – and whose material status is thereby all the more obviously superior.

Often, finding little satisfaction in their occupational lives, people turn for their personal fulfilment to their family engagements. The family itself is a context in which questions about time in human life seem particularly relevant. It is also a context in which the experience of the two genders is likely to be very different. As such, we shall be looking quite closely at the family in two later chapters. Here, it seems important to consider one particular question about the place of family engagements in the lives of adults. That is, the gains and losses of those who do, and who do not establish their own family units.

It has been suggested already that marriage and parenthood are widely regarded as crucial marks of reaching true adulthood, true maturity. In this, official psychology very much endorses conventional wisdom. Though there is rather little writing on 'life-span developmental psychology', what books do exist all agree in defining these as the major growth points of adult life up to middle age. These widely held and 'scientifically validated' assumptions must themselves act powerfully on everyone living in our society. *Not* to marry, *not* to have children, is in some sense to declare oneself deviant, apart, other. As we shall see later, the meaning of this deviance is not quite the same for men as for women. At this point, though, we need to consider what the situation may actually entail for the way individual adults experience this phase of their lives.

Obviously, to maintain a way of life which is different to the one generally expected – and generally adopted – in our society, is to be seen as 'different'. But not to marry, and, still more, not to have children, also means, in some sense, never being recognized as fully adult – a proper grown-up. This is, of course, a very denigrating judgment – one which people are likely to resist as far as they can. For adults without families it becomes more urgent, perhaps, than for most people to *prove* their right to be regarded as adults, to take their place within the adult social world. We generally see the tasks of adult life as being to *get on*. Getting on means different things in different adults' lives; it is usually different for men and for women, and it is also probably different for those with and without families. For people who are unmarried and childless, the need to demonstrate visible progress, to be seen to have achieved, to have climbed, may seem particularly important.

Defining and living one's life in these terms is likely to entail some sense of being driven. Through strong inner strivings, people may indeed achieve much, and win widespread social respect and emulation. But such achievements are personally costly. It is not just that being perpetually driven to achieve greater heights is stressful, and makes it difficult to feel serene, at peace with oneself. It is also that the achievements one strives for so urgently – the delicious fruits of success – may themselves turn to ashes in the mouth. Paradoxically, success may be hard to live with, to live up to. It may impose a sense of personal loneliness. And, having reached the topmost pinnacle, what more is there to work for, and where can one go but down?

If adults without families are prone to this sense of the meaning of time in their lives, those who establish their own families may be liable to a different kind of trap. In our conventional wisdom and in official psychology, adulthood is supposed to mean *settling down*. Whereas in adolescence individuals are expected to experiment, try out a variety of things, test for themselves different ways of living – in becoming adult, very different expectations apply. Adult maturity is defined in terms of a life-long commitment to a particular role in life, a particular outlook, a particular life-style. This is probably especially the case in the sphere of family life, where adult members may feel complicated pressures. Parents with teenage children who see them, with pity or contempt, as middle-aged, stagnating, set in their ways, still sometimes find that it is those very children who react with the greatest protest, the greatest outrage, to their attempts at new personal departures, and by doing so, effectively forestall them.

From the perspective of childhood, adult life is a time of freedom. And surely it is adulthood, of all life phases, to which we grant the greatest social autonomy. Economically, adult people have relative independence. As a group, they are not subject to daily institutional control. Many adults not merely possess a good deal of power over their own lives, they also have a large measure of control over those of others. Yet despite all this, most adult men and women do not seem to feel personally free. This must, most fundamentally, have to do with the way we define the meaning of adult human life.

Many men and women, it has been suggested, feel one of two sets of pressures and constraints. On the one hand, people may feel pushed to get on, to be seen to be making progress, and thereby to prove their adult status. On the other, people may be contained within a definition of adulthood which is in fact a trap, since it fixes them in an essentially static mould. These two kinds of pressure may seem to be opposite. But perhaps they are two sides of the same coin. The idea of getting on, and the idea of settling down, both presuppose that growth and change are essentially linear and unidirectional. They both imply that human life involves settling, as a person, into one particular avenue, one particular channel, within which movment, if it occurs, will be forward.

One of the features of this view of adult life is that it assumes that the positive things, the satisfactions and fulfilments, in men's and women's lives will all be of the same order, and will be the product of their position, as adults, in the human life-span. But adult people often seem to experience their greatest joys, their deepest happiness, through their involvements in aspects of life that are not conventionally 'adult'.

If we think about adults in relation to children, one of the most striking differences seems to be that of play. Most children play a lot, and without any apparent difficulty. In playing, they generally seem to have a great deal of fun, they are often very inventive and creative, and they are apt to become totally absorbed in what they are doing. This is very unlike most grown-up people. Many men and women hardly seem able to play at all, or only to play in very deliberate, stilted or self-conscious ways, without any of the delight, the spontaneity of childish games. Perhaps all this is not very surprising. We define children's lives as unserious, adults' as essentially serious. As grown-up people, most of us probably find it hard to lay aside the burden of that seriousness, that purposefulness – the heavy responsibility that, as adults, we carry.

Yet many men and women find themselves able, at least temporarily, to re-enter the world of childhood through their close engagement with children. As the mother of a young child, a woman does not merely come to witness a childish view of the world: she herself *experiences*, in her intimate contact with her daughter, something of the freshness, the wonder, the delight of living as a child – as well as the keenness of childish griefs and troubles.

Nor is it only through engagements with children themselves that adults may sometimes briefly cease to 'be' adults – and thereby nourish and enrich their sense of their own lives. Where relationships between grown-up people are particularly satisfying, particularly fulfilling, this seems to be because those involved are able to do things together for their own sake, not for any more serious purpose. Each person may also, at times, 'be' a child to the other's adult. We all need to be cared for, to be looked after, to be comforted. Although we think of being 'parented' as something to which only children are entitled, through their childishness, an adult life which precludes any others from taking care of oneself is likely to be bleak.

Conventional thinking measures adulthood by contrast with childhood, and implies that, *within* adult life, progress means moving ever further away from childishness. This essentially linear view does not really square at all with what we have just considered. Rather than expecting the fulfilment of adults, as adults, to derive from their separation from childhood, it seems to make better sense to view fulfilled adult life as interpenetrated with childish life. If this is so, we have also to ask how the adult phase of life stands towards later life – the period of old age.

Throughout our lives we carry, at least potentially, an awareness of both our past and our future. The way we constitute things in our society probably means that, for most people, there is a forward orientation in childhood, and a backward one in old age. What happens in adulthood itself? Given that adults are generally expected to prove their maturity in their twenties and thirties – by finding permanent work, marrying, making a home, having children – it is probably within this period that men and women live most intensely in the present. The compelling drive to get on may still keep many men, in particular, oriented towards the future while, as parents, perhaps some people live a good deal in the anticipation of their children's future. Probably few adults, however, dwell more than they must in the prospect of their own old age.

Adult lives differ in the extent to which they involve any engagement with old people. Where this occurs, it is probably most often for those individuals, particularly women, who care for their own parents. Just as it is possible for adults who are engaged with the young to separate themselves psychologically from the children they deal with, so the different roles played by the elderly and those looking after them make the same separation possible. And probably many more people *do* make such an inner separation from the old than do so in relation to the young. The alternative seems, for many people, to be the painful, dreaded realization: is it to this that I must come? Yet this perspective, as already suggested, is based on a very limited view of what it means to be old. By contrast, allowing oneself to feel empathy with an elderly person can mean broadening and enriching one's own sense of life. The last phase of life can sometimes be seen to entail possibilities of maintaining, in another guise, that which is most deeply significant. And if we can allow ourselves sometimes to contemplate this phase, we may more easily escape the vicious treadmill, or the stagnant pool to which adult lives seem so often to be reduced.

6 'DEVIANT' LIVES

Some years ago, an American psychologist named Stanley Schachter* carried out a series of experiments on the psychological effects of drugs. In these experiments, people acting as subjects were injected with substances which they were told would probably produce an alteration of their mood. This happened in groups of about twelve people; what the subjects did not know was that the other eleven were not actually subjects, but trained stooges. Unlike the true subjects, who were injected with genuinely psychotropic substances, the stooges – who were there to act a prearranged part – received only saline solution. Following the injections, after a little while one or two of the stooges would begin to act out a particular mood – voicing a sense of frustration at the situation, for instance, shouting angrily at the experimenter, perhaps even threatening violence. Gradually, other stooges followed suit, expressing similar feelings of rage and irritability. In another group, the mood portrayed would be that of depression; the stooges would assume attitudes of dejection or despair, weep, express sadness, hopelessness. In a third group, the picture might be that of elation, with the stooges talking gaily, animatedly, moving about a good deal, laughing freely. In all these groups, the prearranged mood to be acted out was at variance with the nature of the drug the one true subject had actually received. So the subject injected with a depressant drug would find herself in a group of others all apparently experiencing irritation and anger. Or someone whose injection had been of an anger-producing drug would see others, appar-

* Schachter, S. and Singer, J.E. (1962), Cognitive, social and physiological determinants of emotional state, *Psychological Review*, 69, 379–99.

ently similarly injected, in a state of obvious elation. And so on.

In these peculiar situations, what happened to the genuine subjects? Strangely, the 'effects' they felt the drug having were not those which, biochemically, they *should* have felt. Instead, the feelings produced – actually *experienced* by these subjects – were those being expressed by others who seemed to be in the same boat. The person in whose bloodstream ran a substance 'known' to produce elation did not feel the least sense of elation; on the contrary, he felt inexplicably sad and depressed, just like all those around him. It was obvious to him that, like his fellow-subjects, he must have been injected with a depressant drug. In unfamiliar physical situations, where they are unsure just what to expect, people do, it seems, define what is happening to them by reference to the reactions of others – rather than by what is actually taking place physiologically. This suggests that even in the privacy of our own bodies – in the events that take place inside our own skins – we still look to others to tell us what it is that we are feeling.

This is, perhaps, merely an extreme version of a theme which runs throughout our lives. A new teacher arrives one morning to take over your class. She is not like the previous one – quite different, in fact, from any of the teachers you have met before. She looks different, she approaches you differently, she talks in a way that is unfamiliar. What are you to make of her? How should you act towards her? In order to know this, you must have recourse to others in the class. How are other children reacting to her, receiving her? From their response, you can begin to get some sense of the kind of person she is, and the kinds of position towards her that are appropriate for you to take. Or perhaps, as you travel to work as usual, the tube train stops in the tunnel between stations. Time goes on, it still does not move; half an hour passes. Is this the start of a catastrophe? You cannot really tell, except from the way that others in the carriage are reacting. Perhaps they just go on calmly sitting there. Even though some people look ostentatiously at watches, sigh loudly, shake their heads, or offer sympathetic smiles – still, it is obvious that the situation does not call for panic, is no more than a nuisance. But suppose your fellow-travellers begin to show signs of real terror – suppose that some people scream, others try desperately to force open the doors, to break the glass of the windows, or pull the emergency handle over and over again? If this happened, you might find yourself feeling sensations of real anxiety, real panic. The situation would instantly have been transformed into a terrifying crisis.

In unfamiliar, ambiguous, unpredictable situations, situations where we feel at a loss, other people give us a kind of purchase on things. Through our reference to others, we can get a sense of what the situation means, and therefore, of what ideas, feelings, reactions may be appropriate. The reference function which, as human beings, we hold for each other is essentially to assure ourselves about the positions, the stances, that we should take. As such, it does, of course, extend far more widely than merely novel or emergency situations; its reach, perhaps, covers the whole of our lives. Constantly, in countless automatic and unacknowledged ways, we refer to others to define our own position. At a social gathering, you notice your skirt is long compared to those of other women; instantly, you realize you are out of fashion. Talking to a new acquaintance, you begin to feel a slightly shameful sense of superiority; it seems he only rents his house, whereas you own yours. Your ten-year-old friend tells you she has just got a bicycle; though you never thought of it before, you now see that you must have one too. Or when your father remarks 'By the time I was your age . . .' you feel an urgent need to prove that you can get as far as he did, or further.

The recourse we make, in situations like these, is not to just anybody, but to those who are felt to be comparable with us, to be like ourselves. For children trying to figure out a new teacher, the attitude of the deputy head, who introduces her to the class, is of no relevance. It is other children's reactions which are critical. Conversely, for adult people in the stationary tube train, how any children present react is immaterial; it is the responses of other adults which are felt to have personal implications for themselves. And among such adults, those who are seen as most closely comparable to oneself are particularly important. The middle-aged businessman puts down the woman's screams to female hysteria, while seeing the young man's battering of the door as youthful loss of control – but lurches into panic when the middle-aged man sitting opposite begins to shout wildly, seizes hold of his neighbour, is visibly desperate.

Age plays a major role in our sense of others as reference groups, reference figures, for ourselves. The lives of other people whom we see as developmentally comparable represent a kind of standard against which we judge our own lives. We engage in endless matchings of ourselves with others at the same stage. We use others to evaluate our own competence, achievements, possessions, personal standing; only if we are as good as – or preferably better than – they are, can we be satisfied with our own performance. In little ways, we constantly monitor our peers to know how we ourselves are doing. And more fundamentally, we take their lives as the criterion against which we measure our own – to judge whether we should reproach or congratulate ourselves for what our lives add up to.

In all this, there is, of course, an implicit assumption that age has a standard significance – or at least, one that is standard for males and one that is standard for females. And many of our judgments make explicit reference to this. It was all right her being such a tomboy when she was little, but by now, she should be taking an interest in her appearance, and in boys. At his age, he ought to have decided what he is going to do with his life. That boy should have learned not to cry; after all, he is nearly eight years old. Surely at his time of life, he ought not to be such a rolling stone – he should have settled down by now. Sometimes, the implications of age are seen as inverse. It's disgusting, at her age, to be flaunting her body like that. Or, those five-year-olds couldn't possibly have any racial prejudices; they're much too young for that sort of thing.

The assumption that time has such a general kind of significance in human life runs very deep in conventional wisdom and in official psychology. What we define as *normal* derives from the way we expect people to change with age. In the life periods considered in the last three chapters, the 'normal' shape of human life is essentially that of an inverted U – getting there, having arrived, falling away. Critical to this view, it has been suggested, is our idea of adult maturity – of what it is to arrive. We expect that adults, as adults, will be people of some *substance*. If they are to be seen as normal, they must have clearly established themselves in some recognizable and acceptable life pattern. They must own things, possess a material solidity. They must carry responsibilities, rather than themselves being dependent on others. Essentially they must amount to something.

In a novel entitled *Housekeeping*, Marilynne Robinson speaks as Ruthie, living, together with her sister Lucille, under the care of her aunt, Sylvie, after their mother's suicide. Lucille, armed with dress patterns, nail polish and new friends, eventually moves out into the world. But Ruthie becomes drawn gradually into her aunt's strange, shadowy, insubstantial world. As a girl, she compares herself with her sister:

> I felt the notice of people all over me, like the pressure of a denser medium. Lucille, impatient with my sorrows, had pried the heels off my shoes to make me shorter, but it seemed to me that without them the toes turned up. At times like this I was increasingly struck by Lucille's ability to look the way one was supposed to look.

Later, her 'differentness' is still more evident:

> We are drifters. And once you have set your foot in that path it is hard to imagine another one. Now and then I take a job as a waitress, or a clerk, and it is pleasant for a while. Sylvie and I see all the movies. But finally the imposture becomes burdensome, and obvious . . . when the customers and the waitresses and the dishwasher and the cook have told me, or said in my hearing, so much about themselves that my own silence seems suddenly remarkable, then they begin to suspect me, and it is as if I put a chill on the coffee by serving it. What have I to do with these ceremonies of sustenance, of nurturing?*

* Robinson, M., *Housekeeping*, Penguin Books, 1981.

By being as they are, people like Ruthie represent a standing affront to our taken-for-granted notions of what adulthood should mean. Because Ruthie can not, or will not, live the kind of life that is 'appropriate' for a grown-up woman, she defies our sense that age means progression. As such, she is not 'normal', since 'normality' demands being a particular kind of person, living a particular sort of life, according to the age we have reached. 'Normal' does, of course, carry the very strongest moral overtones. To be normal is to be a proper sort of person, essentially all right. Not to be normal, to be 'deviant', is to be a problem – wrong. People who find themselves 'deviant' are likely, as Ruthie does, to question themselves anxiously, guiltily, as to how they come to be like that. But it is not only 'deviant' people themselves who feel such anxiety. For those who are 'normal' the very existence of those who are 'not normal' constitutes the deepest kind of threat. 'Deviant' human beings jolt us out of the comfortable sense of reality we share – the reality within which we live, within which our own lives have meaning. It is this reality which, in our constant, habitual, reciprocal reference to each other, we actually constitute together. And it is this reality which people like Ruthie threaten to undermine by refusing to conform – that is, to play their part in this vital mutual confirmation.

If we consider adult people who have been defined as deviant, it seems that in different ways they violate some of our most basic assumptions about what it means to be adult. The two main groups of such people are 'criminals' on the one hand, and the 'mentally ill' on the other; and of these two groups, it is the second whose deviance is more fundamentally challenging, more seriously threatening. Criminal people, on their side, are seen as having 'normal' goals – the material wealth and status to which adults are expected to aspire. They are also generally seen as maintaining – for however perverted a cause – the proper stance of an adult person: that is, they are credited, whether rightly or wrongly, with taking responsibility for themselves – planning, acting purposefully. It is only in the methods they adopt that their deviance consists, because to act criminally is, typically, to take a short cut in order to obtain the rewards more quickly. In this, criminal people violate our expectations that the adult goals may be reached only by certain socially recognized routes (however dubious some of these may be), and they make a mockery of all those other adults who continue, perhaps without much hope, to 'work' for material advancement.

Those who engage in crime may constitute a threat to our notions of proper adult behaviour. But this is nothing compared to the threat posed by those labelled mentally ill. Most basically, such people do not keep up the 'front' that we expect of those who are grown up; instead, they declare, in one way or another, that they cannot cope, cannot manage their lives. Far from maintaining a good face at all costs – as men and women are supposed to do – the mentally ill let their distress spill over, for all to see. Despite their chronological maturity, in 'breaking down' they fail to take responsibility for themselves, and all too clearly need the help, the comfort, the support of other people. Most troubling of all, the reason for their distress is unclear; to be desperately unhappy when you have 'all that a normal woman could ask for' is to put a disturbing question-mark over our taken-for-granted definition of adult life.

Ruthie, in Marilynne Robinson's novel, asks herself how she has come to be so different from other people. If we think of those who, as adults, are 'deviant', it looks as if their 'differences' can usually be traced back to childhood. The schizophrenic woman was autistic as a girl, the persistent thief, a juvenile delinquent, the depressed adult, a maladjusted child. Such histories appear altogether unsurprising. It is no wonder, we are inclined to say, that personal deviance manifests itself in pre-adult life, or that peculiar children grow up to be abnormal adults. Yet perhaps these parallels, in childhood and adulthood, mean something rather different from what we usually assume. It may be that they have less to do with any 'innate differences' than with the perceptions of others.

Juvenile delinquents are young people – usually boys – who have been convicted of committing various offences. What are these offences? Typically, they are such acts as petty theft, housebreaking, truancy, vandalism, driving under age, or 'borrowing' a car for a joyride. But there is nothing striking about these delinquent acts, in marking out particular boys over and against others. On the contrary – as a number of psychologists have found – they are, in one form or another, virtually standard behaviour for adolescent boys in our society. Juvenile delinquents, therefore, are not boys or girls who have engaged in atypical, deviant behaviour. They are young people who, as individuals, have been socially sanctioned for committing offences which are very widespread within their age group.

The situation of 'maladjusted' children is very similar. Some years ago, for instance, a British psychiatrist, Michael Shepherd, together with some colleagues, examined a number of children who had been sent to Child Guidance Clinics.* In order to see how abnormal these children's behaviour was, Shepherd and his colleagues also examined an equal number of children, of the same age and from the same schools and neighbourhoods, who had never been referred to such clinics. In this comparison, no differences emerged. The 'normal' children, it turned out, had just as many 'problems' as the 'maladjusted' ones. For every clinic child who wet his bed, had temper tantrums, worried over school work, could not get on with other children, suffered night terrors, was disruptive or aggressive – for every child like this, there were equal numbers who had never been referred, never come to be 'diagnosed' maladjusted.

If children defined as normal, on the one hand, and delinquent or maladjusted on the other, seem not to be so very different, this basic comparability does not last long. These are fateful labels. To be publicly termed delinquent, to be diagnosed disturbed – this is to set your foot on the long path of a deviant life career. Our social 'treatment' of what we view as abnormality, so far from 'curing' it, tends to act to ensure its life-long perpetuation. While most boys 'grow out' of their delinquency, those who are convicted by the courts and sent to special community

* Shepherd, M., Oppenheim, B. and Mitchell, S., *Childhood Behaviour and Mental Health*, University of London Press, 1971.

homes or borstals generally do not. Their institutionalization, while providing a 'school for crime', also forestalls any other kinds of social engagement, and places a stigma on their future social standing. And, just as juvenile delinquents usually go on to become adult criminals, so disturbed, maladjusted children tend to end up as adults prone to mental illness. Again, the effect of removal from ordinary school, of experiencing special, different kinds of treatment and institutions is essentially stigmatizing; as such, it demoralizes, it undermines confidence in oneself as an ordinary boy or girl among others.

As deviant careers progress, things typically become much worse. Few people would maintain that the prisons where adult criminals are incarcerated have any real potential for remedying their criminal tendencies. Psychiatric hospitals, on the other hand, are expected to be therapeutic. Yet for those on 'chronic' wards – as I know from first-hand experience – daily life is one of dreary routine, devoid of personal dignity and human relationships. Even for those whose passage through hospital is briefer, or takes the form of out-patient treatment, there remains the huge stigma of being a 'mental case'; it is a fact which those involved take care not to disclose to strangers – a fact apt to strike a sudden chill if it happens to 'come out'.

All this suggests that, so far from treating, remedying, curing deviance, the way we cater for it actually consolidates and perpetuates it. In our terror at what seems abnormal, we exclude certain people from our ordinary society – and thereby confirm and crystallize their 'otherness'. Perhaps, therefore, we should look as carefully as we can at what is essentially involved in the threat which being deviant seems to carry.

The generality of delinquent behaviour among adolescent boys has already been remarked, as has the fact that children diagnosed as maladjusted do not have any more, or any different, problems from those defined as normal. What distinguishes the children who come to be labelled deviant from those who do not, is evidently not their own idiosyncratic behaviour, but rather the attitudes of people who are in contact with them. A child of eight cannot settle to sleep without a lengthy bedtime ritual – though her younger brothers and sisters have long ago learned to dispense with such things. For some parents, this falls well within the bounds of what is acceptable, understandable, behaviour. But for others, it does not. She should have grown out of this by now. There must be something wrong with her – we shall have to take her to see someone. What is it that enables some parents – and others – to take a larger view of the lives around them, while others are more easily afraid of behaviour that is different?

In trying to answer this question, perhaps we should consider a third form of human deviance – that of mental handicap. People who are defined as mentally handicapped do, in a very obvious way, represent a challenge to our psychology of development. They do not grow up in the same sense as other children. Often they do not learn to take care of themselves in ordinary ways, to be responsible for their own dressing, feeding, personal care – let alone learning to read and write, or acquiring the other skills of school. As adults, they remain dependent, sometimes on parents, more usually on hospital. While other men and women are earning their own living, maintaining their own households, bringing up their own families, mentally handicapped adults are typically sitting, eating, sleeping, in special segregated institutional wards. And if psychiatric hospitals suffer a low status in the National Health Service, mental handicap hospitals represent still more of a Cinderella. Lacking financial resources, suffering chronic staff shortages, housed in antiquated buildings, such institutions often fail to provide even adequate physical care. Again, I can speak from my own experience of the dismalness of life for hospital inmates; as one patient commented, 'They think we've got no feelings, but we're human beings.' This treatment is, it seems, the public expression of the repugnance which many individuals feel towards those who are mentally handicapped.

In a thoughtful book entitled *The Politics of Mental Handicap*,* a British psychologist, Joanna Ryan, discusses the situation of those who suffer mental handicap. She considers the attitudes

---

* Ryan, J. and Thomas, F., *The Politics of Mental Handicap*, Penguin Books, 1980.

of contempt and rejection which such people typically experience in our society, both in and out of hospital. These contrast markedly with the genuine acceptance and affection felt towards the mentally handicapped by those who work with them in religious communities. It is, Ryan suggests, only when mentally handicapped people are truly accepted for what they are – rather than for the hope of the limited progress they might achieve in 'normalization' programmes – that it becomes possible to value them as human beings. Only if those around them can stop trying desperately, hopelessly, to push them on towards being 'normal' will their real qualities – of emotional responsiveness, lack of inhibition, absence of hypocrisy – be evident.

As Ryan remarks, mentally handicapped people 'strain our sense of humanity'. It is difficult, really to accept as fully human, those who are in some ways so different from ourselves. People who do not seem to develop, who, as adults, cannot lead what we think of as adult lives – these people do constitute a threat to our idea of human progression. Yet by the same token, they can remind us of the limits of that idea. It is in the competitive arenas of formal schooling, paid work, material progress that the mentally handicapped have no place. And ultimately, our sense of the scope of our lives, the goals of our development, must move beyond these things.

Mentally handicapped people are most threatening, perhaps, because their existence lays open to question the individualistic and competitive values which underpin so much in our society. And perhaps it is because other deviant people also implicitly question certain fundamental values that we find it necessary to put them out of sight. Criminals, it may be, show up the hypocrisy, the falsity of our entrepreneurial mentality; in a sense, they call our bluff. The mentally ill, more fundamentally still, confront us with the pain and insecurity that are inescapable in human existence. In doing so, they cut the ground from under our desperate, precarious mutual assurances that, in adulthood, we can secure for ourselves all that we need – that life itself can be finally arranged and buttoned up. By refusing to live out our conventional psychology, such people act as living testimony to its hollowness, and thereby endorse what, more deeply, we know, but often fear to acknowledge. Yet if we could stop so desperately defending ourselves against this awareness, we should, perhaps, find our lives altogether less brittle.

7 LIVES AS SOCIALLY CONSTRUCTED

In the last chapter we considered how 'deviant' life courses may be the product of others' perceptions, rather than the direct expression of the intrinsic characteristics of those involved. Such perceptions are part of the expectations with which we are all constantly surrounded – the air we daily breathe. These expectations, which govern how we perceive and respond to each other, must surely be very powerful. And because, in our society, we expect life courses to be greatly influenced by features such as class, race and gender, these social categories may play an important part in the way individuals come to shape their personal destinies. It is with social expectations such as these that this chapter is concerned.

During the late 1960s, two groups of teenage youths lived in the suburbs of an American city. William Chambliss, the sociologist who studied them,* dubbed them the Saints and the Roughnecks. Both groups spent their days in characteristic ways. On weekdays, the eight Saints regularly went truant from school; but this was seldom noticed because they had developed techniques for covering their absence by apparently legitimate reasons. Their days were spent in a cafe or a pool hall, both some distance from their own neighbourhood. On Friday and Saturday nights the Saints would drive into the city and drink heavily in taverns or nightclubs. They then drove around the streets, looking for possibilities. If they found an empty house, they would break in, smash up the furniture and windows, urinate on the walls, or scrawl obscenities. When they saw a road repair site,

* Chambliss, W. J., 'The Saints and the Roughnecks', in *Readings in Adolescent Psychology: Contemporary Perspectives*, ed. Cottle, T. J., Harper and Row, 1977.

they would remove the barricades and wait to see an unsuspecting motorist drive into the open hole. Or they would place the stolen barricade at a spot where motorists could not avoid crashing into it. Despite these escapades, performed in the context of heavy drinking under age, and of drunken and reckless driving, this behaviour never resulted in serious injury, and the Saints were very seldom stopped by the police. On the rare occasions where this occurred, they would appear contrite and apologetic, and no further action would be taken. The Saints were, in fact, generally regarded as good boys, who might occasionally indulge in a little high-spirited fun. All of them were successful in school, and were well regarded by their teachers, even though they were seen as achieving less than their full potential. To the local community, the boys were essentially solid young citizens, with respectable futures ahead of them.

With the Roughnecks, things were rather different. The six youths in this gang were viewed, at school and in the neighbourhood, as boys in trouble, and destined for trouble. Unlike the Saints, who had nice homes, good manners, expensive clothes, these boys did not own cars or possess much money. As a result, they were restricted in their leisure time to their own neighbourhood – a crowded urban area where they were highly visible to members of their community, including teachers and police. In this local context, they had come to be regarded as a rough delinquent gang, always hanging around the drug store, and being a nuisance to passers-by. Yet, in fact, their delinquent activities were much more sporadic than the regular offences of the Saints, and consisted mainly in petty theft and occasional fighting on the part of one or two members. When it came to school, the six Roughnecks, though they saw their schooling as a burden, did not actually truant, but were regular attenders. Nevertheless, they generally achieved poor results and were seen by their teachers as problem pupils. This reputation was echoed in the judgment of their local community, where they were constantly involved with the police who, though seldom catching them in theft, tended to harass them for loitering.

These two groups of boys were, objectively, both delinquent.

Of the two gangs, it was the misdeeds of the Saints which were, objectively, the more numerous and the more serious. Yet it was the other gang, the Roughnecks, which was viewed by its society as a group of tough young criminals, while the Saints were regarded as normal, upstanding young citizens. Such different judgments in youth carry, of course, very different predictions of the kinds of adult life to be expected. And in their future careers, these two groups did live out the differential predictions made for them.

Within the complex of factors which govern our life courses, the way that, in youth, we come to be socially defined, must have significant impact. As Chambliss himself argues, the anti-social activities in which certain young men engage in our society get noticed, while those of others do not. In general, where those involved are middle class, have good manners, reputations, and are well off enough to leave their own neighbourhoods for the wild oats they sow – in this situation, delinquent acts will tend to be invisible. Leaving their delinquency behind them as they enter the socially expected respectability of their adult careers, these individuals may look back fondly at the pranks of their youth. But things are likely to turn out very differently for delinquents who are working class. Highly visible within their locality, publicly labelled and sanctioned in youth for their misdeeds, it surprises nobody that such individuals move into deviant adult careers that are entirely consistent with their deviant adolescence.

This process is, of course, the one with which we were concerned in the last chapter. It is the process whereby differential social reactions may themselves help to create 'normal' or 'deviant' life careers. But as the Chambliss study shows, the different forms which social reaction takes are not just a question of the tolerance levels of individuals. In our society, we experience the behaviour of others in the context of their social status, their social group position. It was the middle-class status of the Saints which defined their misdemeanours as essentially harmless pranks, and the working-class status of the Roughnecks which, by contrast, rendered their behaviour criminal. In the life careers into which, as individuals, we are guided, who we are is at least as important as what we do.

Not only does the influence of social status affect who comes to be defined as deviant, and who escapes such definition. Even within the category of deviance, the particular forms of abnormality that are attributed to individuals are influenced by their social categorization. A woman caught shoplifting, for example, is likely to be viewed rather differently from a man caught in the same act. Where the man's theft is simply defined as a criminal offence, requiring penal sanction, the woman's behaviour is generally interpreted in terms of personal pathology. She is reacting to personal stress, perhaps associated with the menopause, her husband's infidelity, or children leaving the nest. Her theft is only the symptom of a deeper kind of emotional disturbance, for which treatment, not punishment, is required. One reason why, as convicted criminals, males so hugely outnumber females and, conversely, why so many more women than men are diagnosed as mentally ill must be that the behaviour of men and women is characteristically interpreted so differently.

When we think about how it is that individuals come to forge such different life courses, we seldom explain things in terms like these. We do not see 'normality' or 'deviance' as being constituted through social interpretation, social reaction, social negotiation. In fact, we do not really think of those involved as individuals in interchange with other individuals. Instead, we regard them merely as representatives of their social class, their race, their gender, and so on. And because such categories seem to carry particular innate psychological directions, our reference to them appears to offer sufficient explanation for the way people behave. Gender, for instance, has – or so we generally believe – a major influence on personality. Because we expect men to be, by nature, aggressive and competitive, we find it altogether unsurprising that they should engage in relatively more crime. Conversely, we expect women to be weaker and more vulnerable than men, and therefore see it as natural that they should outnumber men in statistics of personal disturbance and breakdown. Yet these differences in 'incidence' of particular ways of behaving, while seeming to confirm our thinking about male-female differences, are also themselves influenced by that thinking – may in some sense be the product of it.

Looked at like this, gender may exert its influence on life not directly but through our preconceptions and judgments as to its significance. And, perhaps, this is also true of race. Within our society, the lives of those whose skins are not white are, in general, relatively disadvantaged. Where most white children get through their schooling without any serious disruption, dark-skinned children, particularly those of Afro-Caribbean origin, quite often end up excluded from ordinary schools – relegated to schools for slow learners, or special units for disruptive pupils. Even those who remain in mainstream education leave school without exam certificates much more often than do white-skinned pupils. This, of course, makes them vulnerable to unemployment. But even armed with numerous 'O' levels, young black people seem generally to do badly in the employment market; they characteristically end up in poorly paid, dirty or dead-end jobs. Low status and poor remuneration makes it difficult to obtain good housing, in pleasant neighbourhoods, and so black families tend to congregate in the ghettos of delapidated inner-city areas.

How do we explain these systematic differences between those whose skins are dark or white, at every stage of their human lives? We have, as a rule, no trouble in understanding them. We explain these consistently diverse life courses by reference to the psychological characteristics of black- and white-skinned people. They are, essentially, different kinds of people. There is no question – most of us would say – of one kind being *superior* to the other; they are simply different types. Most basically, the difference is defined as one of motivation. Where white people are generally prepared to work for future goals, to make sacrifices in the here-and-now, black people live more in the present, are less inhibited, more spontaneous. That is why black children tend to under-achieve at school, and do not easily accept the discipline of teachers. The same qualities are seen to underlie the generally poor occupational careers of black adults, their failure to acquire material resources, and their tendency to impulsive social action, such as mugging or street violence. The facts – in educational records, criminal statistics, and social documentation – all seem to prove the validity of this line of explanation. If black people are *not*, as a group, so different psychologically from the rest of us, then why do they feature so prominently in all these forms of social deviance? It seems clear that, taken as a whole, they constitute a distinctive and different kind of group, adapted to the culture of their origin, but less well suited to life in our own society.

In accounting for the way these supposedly basic differences come to exist, most people would probably refer to a combination of childhood learning along with certain innate tendencies. On top of a psychological make-up which, like their black skin, is distinctive to such people, they learn, during their impressionable early years, social norms that value spontaneity and freedom over discipline and control. This learning occurs, above all, within the family. Because these are frequently one-parent, without a continuous father-figure, and because the mother is often out at work, young children, it is argued, grow up lacking a basic sense of restraint and stability. By the time they reach school, they have probably already become the uninhibited, undisciplined prototype of their own social group.

These kinds of explanations locate the disadvantage of black members of our society within their own personalities, rather than within the social expectations and the social treatment they encounter because of their position in society. As such, they serve the function that has been called 'blaming the victim'. The message is that of Butler's Erewhonian judge passing sentence on a man convicted of pulmonary tuberculosis: 'You may say that it is your misfortune, but I answer that it is your crime to be unfortunate.' But we apply similar kinds of explanation much more widely than this. In understanding our own lives, those of friends and acquaintances, the lives of exceptional people, life courses that are tragic or triumphant – in all these, it is to the fixed characteristics of individuals, as individuals, that we habitually resort.

It is the argument of this book that the way we live – the personal journey we make through time – is the outcome of constant, intricate and far-reaching dealings with each other. So far from merely living out a pre-existing personal destiny, carried within our genes, we ourselves construct lives that are viable within our own social contexts. Nor does the process of construction stop when we reach the early years of adulthood. Human beings are not clay, to be moulded, once and for all, into a particular unalterable shape. If individuals often do seem to stop short in their development – to become altogether set in their ways – this is because we live in a society based on a very limited idea of human development and possibility. One consequence of such limits is the restriction of opportunities for older people, making development difficult. But the barriers we all encounter are not just external. As members of a society, we share its collective psychology. It requires courage and imagination to move in one's thinking beyond habitual limits. Yet again, to live out a less cramped, less constraining developmental psychology must involve others. Since as human beings we live in relation to each other, new ways of seeing, of doing, must be socially negotiated.

Just as most people would explain the less privileged lives of black people by reference to certain inborn characteristics, combined with early experience, so our construction of the diverse courses of human life typically makes reference to such innate personal features as gender and physique, and to early experience in families, especially in terms of loss or deprivation. In general, we see the personality of individuals as a complex product of these two kinds of factor. Being born male or female, we generally believe, involves two distinctive sorts of personal heritage. Throughout their lives, males and females will naturally differ. Boys and men will tend to be drawn into instrumental, objective, public spheres of action, girls and women into expressive, private, personal domains. The appropriate, the natural, the normal life course of a man will be that of agency and achievement, while that of a woman will normally have as its central theme the care and support of others. And – as we have seen earlier in this chapter – these themes in the meaning of gender also interpenetrate our view of 'deviance', according to whether a man or woman is involved.

It is gender, too, which sets the context within which physique is accorded significance. At its broadest, physical biology is often seen as carrying particular kinds of tendency – like the spontaneity, the lack of restraint, supposedly common to black people, or perhaps the quick temper, the resonance to music, the mechanical flair reputedly carried in family genes. But even such tendencies as these take their particular meaning within the more basic dimension of gender. And it is this dimension which governs what qualities of physical embodiment are viewed as having significance for the course of human life. For males, size and strength are seen as vital, and weakness, puniness, as serious handicaps. For females, conversely, smallness, daintiness of build are assets rather than liabilities, while good looks and prettiness are the most precious inheritance. Unlike most of the factors that are conventionally supposed to be developmentally crucial, factors of physique are seen as operating in adolescence rather than in early childhood. This is because adult embodiments are not evident until after puberty.

It is, though, during early childhood that people generally see the most crucial, the most far-reaching, the most irreversible kinds of personal moulding as occurring. We tend to believe that – regardless of gender, of physical inheritance – individuals cannot grow up into right kinds of people unless they have had a particular kind of early family experience. To have grown up during the early years in a stable family group, which includes both father and mother – this is seen as the sine qua non of satisfactory later development. Drastic changes during these years, in family group composition, and in particular, the loss of a mother, are thought to produce serious personality damage. In his well known dictum that maternal deprivation, in the first five years of life, produced people who were unable to love, the psychiatrist, John Bowlby, was perhaps merely giving official expression to a belief which was already widely held.* Captured

* Bowlby, J., *Maternal Care and Mental Health*, W.H.O., Geneva, 1951.

in *West Side Story*, by the phrase, 'We're depraved on account of we're deprived', the explanation of later deviance, unhappiness or chaos has long been seen to lie in early family traumas.

Such factors as these must indeed be very significant. In our society – probably in any society – it is a matter of supreme importance whether one is born male or female. Physical features such as body build, skin colour, physical integrity or physical damage – these are seldom merely incidental features in people's lives. As for childhood, there must be few who would not acknowledge the momentous significance, in later life, of the early years, especially within the intimate world of the family. And to have suffered loss, within that intensely personal realm, is to have experienced something whose impact may be devastating and whose reverberations may indeed continue over a lifetime.

Yet if all these things have huge psychological significance, perhaps that significance is not the way we generally understand it. We do, for instance, assume that gender, physique, family upbringing and early loss all have a human meaning which is standard. But there are, as we all know, exceptions. Many lives are now on record which seem triumphantly to disprove the destructiveness of early parental loss, or to transcend the disablement of physical deformity, the confines of gender barriers. Perhaps this should make us reflect on what these things actually mean. Perhaps experience, of itself, carries no standard meaning; it is what we make of our experience which governs the impact it comes to have on us.

Because, in our psychology, both general and official, we tend to see certain features as operating in a standard, universal way, our conception is essentially linear, and mechanistic. We think of human life as getting set, getting permanently programmed, by certain factors present at birth, together with certain factors operating in early childhood. People who have experienced favourable combinations of these factors will, we expect, come out all right; they will have been set on a right kind of life course and, barring catastrophe, nothing that later happens to them will deflect them from it. Conversely, those with adverse innate inheritance and early experience will have been disastrously shaped. Their unsatisfactory future adulthood, their maladjusted life courses, are already created, only waiting to be lived out. However good their later experience may be, nothing can ever reverse that early shaping: the most such people can hope for is to get by, without their personal vulnerability being too keenly exposed. All this does, of course, place the only dynamic of human life within the very early phase of the life-span, while seeing the adult years as merely an arena in which the effects of that early dynamic are played out.

Stories like those of the Saints and the Roughnecks do not seem to fit into this kind of psychological account. They suggest that, far from operating in a mechanistic way, human beings, at every stage of the life cycle, respond to others in shaping their own lives. Just as the Saints and the Roughnecks, despite their comparably delinquent adolescent behaviour, became the two markedly different sets of adults they were socially expected to become – so, perhaps, we all come to constitute our lives through our negotiation with the society we live in. In this, the expectations of others are very powerful. As women, we find the way has been 'cleared' for us to behave in certain ways that are different from those of men; to do otherwise is to meet social incomprehension, to arouse the anxiety, the disapprobation of those around us. Similarly, black members of society produce, in other people, a sense of incongruence if they aim high in life; young black people who say they hope to enter the professions are judged to have inappropriate aspirations for themselves.

Yet this is not just another sort of mechanistic process, whereby we are merely passive objects, subject to the opinions of others, moulded by social expectation. We ourselves are surely active in negotiating our lives with those around us; and it is through that negotiation that we actually constitute them. It is because, typically, we accept, we personally endorse, that we are the kind of human being we are socially viewed to be, that we come to live out our life in ways that are consonant with that identity. Social class, it has been said, is one's *expectation* of being treated by others, with deference on the one hand, or lack of respect on the other. In planning their lives, most middle- and working-class people incorporate such expectations as a matter of course. So, while middle-class parents plan, as a taken-for-granted expectation, a university education for their baby son, this is seldom part of the plan of working-class parents. It is also this incorporation of their own diminishing social identity which allows the elderly to accept, so often, the degradation of their life opportunities.

Within a society such as ours, which consistently differentiates its members on lines of class, race and gender, it is, indeed, very hard to transcend such differential expectations and, for less privileged members, to re-negotiate for themselves a less restricting social identity in the life courses they run. And perhaps this will remain impossible as long as we hold the kind of psychology we do, which attributes different life careers to the innate and irreversible characteristics of individuals. We should, therefore, re-examine the sense we make of our personal lives.

Important though such features as gender, on the one hand, or early experience, on the other, may be, we should not see them as operating in a mechanical way. Instead, we should look as closely and carefully as we can at the meaning we give these features – the place they hold in our collective psychology.

In the first part of this book we examined some of the common assumptions about the meaning of time in human life. So far from representing three qualitatively distinct kinds of human being, it seemed that there are no fundamental distinctions to be found between young, adult and old people. Much the same appeared, on close inspection, to be true in the case of 'deviant' and 'normal' people. Where divergences exist, these seem to be the product of the complex and subtle processes of social negotiation. These processes are themselves anchored in shared beliefs about the meaning of certain factors in human life. It is to the four factors we have just considered – gender, physique, family life, and loss – that we shall now turn. It is important to trace, as far as possible, the significance with which – together with others in our intimate social networks – we endow these spheres of our experience, and thereby make them operate in our lives. And since ultimately that significance itself is woven into the metaphors we use to understand our living, it is with metaphor that the book will end.

8 LIFE AS GENDER

A few years ago I had a letter from a psychologist who worked in Minnesota, U.S.A. He wrote to ask if I would allow him to publish an article I had written previously, in a book of readings he was compiling. I wrote back giving my permission. We then had a correspondence amounting to about four letters on each side; there were various arrangements to be made – abridging the article, gaining the previous publishers' permission, detailing the other contributions, and so on. Then, at this point, my correspondent ended his letter, 'Yours in sisterhood', and I realized that it was a woman I had been writing to. This realization filled me with consternation. I examined all the letters I had received, and tried to remember every detail of what I had written in my own letters. I could not have said just what I was looking for. The series of letters was essentially impersonal and, logically, it should have made no difference that my correspondent was female rather than male. Yet, somehow, this fact made me profoundly uncomfortable; it seemed to undermine the whole position from which I had been writing.

What place should we give such matters when we think of our life careers? In human life, gender is perhaps the single most important aspect of identity. Though it is possible to imagine a person who belonged to no particular ethnic, cultural or social class grouping, or whose age was totally indeterminate, we cannot do this where gender is concerned. Not only do we need people to be clearly *either* male *or* female; their maleness or femaleness seems to represent the fundamental ground for the other things they are. Throughout our lives, we take gender into account, in multiple and intricate ways, in how we experience each other as particular human beings. The meaning of what we do is perhaps never independent of our gender; the report of a pub brawl takes on an entirely different character when we learn that those involved were women. Nor could their baby's gender ever be a matter of indifference to parents. One has only to think how offended a mother is by the stranger who innocently remarks of her week-old baby boy, 'Oh, isn't she pretty!' From the earliest days of life, long before there are any physical signs of gender, other than purely genital ones, young human beings are viewed as unambiguously, permanently, inescapably male or female. It is to their girl, or their boy, that mothers and fathers talk and respond, in ways that are felt to meet, to reflect, their girlishness, their boyishness. As children grow, what they do, how they talk, the modes by which they engage with their lives – all this is experienced, by their families, and by themselves, as their way of fleshing out a particular identity which is either male or female.

In its significance for us, all through our lives, gender is, above all, a *relation between people*. A way of thinking about this is to reflect on how we embody our gender. Finding you must wait for a train, you go into the station waiting room. Two people are there already. They are standing close together, murmuring to each other. There is a difference in their two stances; one stands erect, the other with the body slightly bent and leaning forward. The first person from time to time puts an arm across the shoulders or around the body of the second. As they talk, the second person, whose head inclines a little to one side, frequently looks up into the face of the first who, in contrast, keeps glancing round the room, with a wary, monitoring look. The second person smiles a good deal, and smiles expansively; the first, less often and more briefly. If all other clues to gender were somehow magically eliminated, it would still be perfectly clear to anyone observing this scene that the first person was male and the second, female.

This kind of physical language has been studied in some detail by a sociologist, Erving Goffman. Goffman uses the term 'gender display', and suggests that, in using it, we all continuously 'choreograph' our world by presenting 'a portrait of the relationship of gender' which governs so much of how we live our lives. As Goffman sees it, this kind of display is not an instinctive possession, but is something which, in living, we all somehow come to learn:

> And this is so even though individuals come to employ expressions in what is sensed to be a spontaneous and unselfconscious way, that is, uncalculated, unfaked, natural. . . . what they naturally express is . . . a version of themselves and their relationships at strategic moments – a working agreement to present each other with, and facilitate the other's presentation of, gestural pictures of the claimed reality of their relationship and the claimed character of their human nature.*

Though we do not generally think of gender in these terms – nor reflect on how it permeates our habitual ways of standing, sitting, walking, our small gestures, the automatic physical responses we make to others – nevertheless our growing up to be feminine or masculine clearly encompasses these aspects of our embodiments. Long before they go to school, small children, to whom gender is already supremely important, have assimilated many of its symbolic bodily expressions. But it is essentially the co-ordination, the complementarity, the *relationship* between masculine and feminine expressiveness which they have come to understand. Dressed in her new blue and white nurses' outfit, the little girl still cannot 'be' a nurse without a boy, or someone 'being' a boy, who will take the part of doctor – someone she can assist, to whom she can defer, towards whom she will play a subordinate role.

What we learn as children about our gender, and what it will mean for us in our lives, does, in fact, comprise the *relation* between feminine and masculine. It is not – as both conventional wisdom and official psychology generally portray it – that girls simply learn how to be feminine, while boys are learning how to be masculine. In some sense, both sexes learn both parts. This is

* Goffman, E., *Gender Advertisements*, Macmillan, 1976.

illustrated by an interesting experiment which was carried out by a British psychologist, David Hargreaves.* He decided to use 'the Circles test' – a series of circular shapes which children are asked to take as the basis for their own drawings, and to draw as many different objects, based on these circles, as they can think of. When boys and girls do this, they usually produce drawings of different sorts of objects – boys typically drawing mechanical objects, for instance, while girls often draw flowers or other natural objects. What Hargreaves did was to ask a number of nine- to eleven-year-old children to do the drawings as though they were a member of the opposite sex; so girls did the test pretending to be boys, and boys, as though they were girls. What happened, when the children played out this pretence, was that they generally produced very accurate representations of the relevant sorts of objects. Boys drew flowers, with much care and detail; girls depicted wheels, putting in the right number of nuts and spokes. Each sex showed an expert knowledge of the realm belonging to the other – a realm which, according to our usual thinking about gender, should have been unknown territory, a closed book. The implication seems to be that, in some sense, girls know how to be boys, and boys, how to be girls.

In the relation between being male and being female, time plays a major part. Many couples expecting their first baby hope that it will be a boy; somehow it feels to them right that the oldest child should be male. Perhaps this is one version of a major theme which runs through our male-female relations: that in man-woman couples, the man should be the older. The few years' seniority that, so typically, husbands have over their wives, is something everyone takes for granted; eyebrows are raised only when the situation is the other way round. And in fact much larger age differences, between men and women, are generally seen as acceptable. Marriages, or affairs, between middle-aged men and young women, are treated as commonplace, natural, only to be expected. Yet a woman of fifty who married a man of twenty-two would find herself the centre of disapproving com-

* Hargreaves, D.J., et al. (1981), Psychological androgyny and ideational fluency, British Journal of Social Psychology, 20, 33–55.

ment – labelled a baby-snatcher, perhaps, even a nympho-
maniac.

One aspect of this view of male-female relations is, in fact, our
sense of the differential significance of time for the sexuality of
men and women. It is not just that we expect males to be older
than females in heterosexual relationships. This is part of a
perception of men in which age does not cancel out sexual life,
may even, up to a point, enhance it. For women, on the other
hand, the progression of time is felt to detract from sexuality.
Where most people would expect men to retain their sexual
interests, and perhaps their sexual activity, throughout their
lives, this expectation does not generally apply to women who,
after the menopause, are often seen as losing their sexual status
altogether. In men, the marks of age are regarded by many as
physically attractive; they denote the positive qualities of 'experience', 'maturity'. But if a women is to be seen as attractive, she
must look young – in order to be sexy, she has to be something of
a 'dolly bird'.

In male-female relations – at least in intimate ones – we feel
that the man should be older, wiser, more experienced than the
woman. In the specifically sexual aspects of the relationship, we
see the man's seniority as still more crucial. All this implies a
model of relations between men and women which is very much
like that of adults with children – the man mature, and the
woman childlike. And perhaps, to be a 'proper woman', one
must remain essentially a child. If we think of all the ways in
which children themselves are encouraged to act appropriately to
their gender, many of them seem to refer to qualities that we view
as childish. It is boys who are reproved for weeping, for clinging
to mother, for not standing up for themselves. To girls, all these
things are allowed, are seen as natural. And in adulthood, though
they may take different forms, the same basic qualities will be
viewed as properly womanly. Women are *expected* to be easily
hurt, easily upset, and to express their feelings freely. This is
part of their 'emotionality' – the quality which makes them so
intuitive, so unable to analyse things rationally, or be objective.
Such features are seen as implying vulnerability; women need

protecting by men and, because of this need, are expected to adopt a submissive, deferential role towards them. This all adds up to a mode of life which is intrinsically less weighty, less serious, than that of men; we think of women's lives as altogether lighter, more frivolous, less weighed down by the important responsibilities of the world.

When these gender-related qualities are stated so baldly, they do, of course, read like a caricature. It seems doubtful whether things can ever really have been like that; and surely now, when the women's movement is so influential, such a picture is massively outdated? Yet, in the *relation* of which gender essentially consists, these very qualities continue to define the differential directions which males and females are expected to take. There can be little doubt that the processes by which children are guided towards their 'own' gender role, and away from that of the 'opposite' gender, are part of the very air they breathe, from the moment of birth onward. This is illustrated by the enormous difficulties encountered by parents who try to bring up children free from the constraints of conventional gender roles. Unless they ban all picture books and comics from the house, unless they forbid the child to watch television, clear messages will come across about what is right for little girls, but not for little boys, or what fathers can, but mothers cannot do. If the child is not to learn such messages from other children, then encounters must be closely monitored; the scorn of friends who see a small boy playing 'girls' games' is likely to be very powerful. And once a child begins to go to school, things become still more difficult. How is it possible to avoid the implications of the traditional books and materials of learning, the pressures of other children, or the differential expectations of the teacher who always asks the boys to help her move the heavy tables, and the girls to tidy up the classroom and arrange the flowers?

In practice, certainly by middle childhood, the worlds of boys and girls are likely to be very different. And this is not only a matter of contrasting games, interests and activities, of the domestic and childcare tasks given to girls, the errands and outside chores assigned to boys, or the tighter controls on

daughters than on sons. Most fundamentally, it involves a particular relationship between the world of girls and the world of
boys. Though little children of three and four may play happily
together, regardless of gender, this soon begins to change; by
seven, at least, there is a mutually agreed separation. Nor does
this just involve segregation; there is often also a sense of mutual
mistrust, mutual antagonism. In accord with the male and female
stereotypes, it is boys who, in this relationship of antagonism,
take up the overtly aggressive stance, while the girls adopt more
passive, fearful stances. In classrooms, to ridicule the efforts of
girls meets the approval, the applause of other boys; in the
playground it is quite routine for a boy casually to disrupt a girls'
careful game as he saunters by.

As boys and girls grow towards adolescence, they necessarily
concern themselves with their own sexuality. Sexuality, too, is
part of the differentiated worlds to which we expect males and
females to belong. As many people have said, women tend to
place sexuality within the context of a loving and affectionate
relationship, where men are apt to view it as an activity in its own
right – an activity through which to 'conquer', to dominate, to
prove themselves. These essentially incompatible expectations,
and the difficulties they can bring young people establishing
heterosexual relationships and perhaps later marrying, are the
subject of a study by Stevi Jackson entitled *Children and Sexuality*.
As she writes:

> Children in our society grow up wary of the opposite sex.
> Long before this mutual suspicion is incorporated into
> sexual relationships, they learn to conform to ideals of
> femininity and masculinity that would make it difficult
> enough for them to like and trust each other even if power,
> male dominance and female subordination did not enter
> the picture. Girls and boys develop opposed values, atti-
> tudes, emotions and behaviour, and yet are expected to
> unite as adults to establish a lasting bond in marriage, an
> institution based very firmly on sexuality. . . . It is in
> childhood that we begin to travel along the paths that lead

to this gulf between men and women. There we begin to mistrust each other and to learn to be the dominated or dominant partner in sexual relationships.*

There are, unfortunately, indications that many husbands and wives fail in their marriages to bridge this 'gulf between men and women'. One of the features contributing to this gulf must be the sheer *differentness* that can exist between the lives of husband and wife. Motherhood, bringing up small children, do, of course, involve many possibilities of personal fulfilment. But they involve other things too. The boredom, the loneliness, the endless drudgery of many women's lives have now been widely documented, and are encapsulated in phrases such as captive wife, or housebound housewife. Alongside such a life may be that of a husband whose life is essentially lived outside the house – and who perhaps sees his wife's daily household care, her childcare, her personal care of him, as the very least he can expect, as representing small compensation for his own daily difficulties, responsibilities, frustrations. Studying the proneness to depression of many married working-class women living in Camberwell, London, George Brown and Tirril Harris came to the conclusion that one of the pressures leading women to breakdown was the lack of communication with husbands.† Where there is mutual incomprehension between two adults living intimately together, the daily stresses, disappointments, anxieties of an economically pressured life cannot be confided, cannot be shared; the tension builds up to levels that are, in the end, unendurable.

Yet things are not always as bad as this. Gender need not always act divisively in the lives of men and women. Brown and Harris met some Camberwell women for whom the concern, the understanding, the support of their husbands had made it possible to surmount major family crises. Somehow, many people do manage to adopt a stance towards life which is not

---

* Jackson, S., *Children and Sexuality*, Blackwell, 1982.
† Brown, G.W. and Harris, T., *Social Origins of Depression*, Tavistock, 1978.

stereotypically male or female or, more often perhaps, manage, through personal struggle, to free themselves from many of the constraints of acting as a feminine or masculine prototype. During childhood, the attitudes of parents must of course be crucial; even if it is impossible to counter all the other pressures towards being 'a proper girl' or 'a real little man', nevertheless, mothers and fathers can convey at least the possibility of other ways of living. Perhaps, too, the relationships which children have with brothers and sisters are fundamental in this. It is strange that little attention is usually given to these relationships. George Eliot's *The Mill on the Floss* evokes powerful resonances for many people who have grown up in families of boys and girls; one can readily enter into Maggie's passionate love of Tom, her yearning for his approval, her anguish at his rejection.

In their impact on later life, brother-sister relationships can be important; yet in official psychology, they remain very much in the background. There is an exception to this, however, in the work of the German psychologist, Walter Toman.* It is Toman's argument that through our childhood relationships with brothers and sisters, we learn the most fundamental aspects of our life-long position towards males and females. Within these relation-ships, he believes, age plays a crucial part. A girl whose brother is older learns that males are stronger, wiser, more competent than females; consequently, she adopts attitudes that are essentially submissive and deferential towards the boys and men she encounters throughout her life. If she marries – so runs Toman's argument – all will go well if her husband happens to be older than any of his sisters. But supposing he grew up with an older sister. In that case, his position towards females will be one of subservience; he will expect the woman to take the major decisions, to carry the greater responsibility, to act as the domi-nant partner. In these circumstances, mutually contradictory expectations will probably ruin the relationship; and Toman claims that statistics about the composition of marriages that break down support such a conclusion. Toman's account does, of

* Toman, W., *Family Constellation*, 1972.

course, treat gender relations – between brothers and sisters and between husbands and wives – in terms of the dimension of dominance and submission. Yet perhaps it is precisely those brother-sister relationships which progress beyond this dimension, and achieve a real richness and intimacy, that may pave the way for relationships between men and women that do not play out traditional, constrained and personally costly gender roles.

If we try to envisage the whole course of human life, it seems that the shape of living can be very different for females and for males. Whereas time is relatively linear, relatively progressive for boys and men, this does not seem to be true for girls and women, who are likely to experience both more discontinuity and instead of a progression, a long plateau in which time may be marked rather than lived. Both boys and girls look forward to their adulthood; both, in some sense, are busily preparing for it, are climbing the slope towards being grown up. But where the path the boys are following goes steadily up, in a more or less straight line, the girls' path changes direction at certain points. Like many climbers, young men find, when they have reached what, as children, they thought was the top, that a further slope confronts them, a slope on which the path continues in much the same direction as the one they took during childhood. For young women, things are probably seldom like this. Not only may the view from the peak look rather different from what they expected; it may also seem that there is really nowhere to go on to from there.

In our society, the goals of males and females are likely to be differently located within the life-span. In general, men are expected to 'achieve' in some sense; and this is something which is not tied to any particular life stage, which can be added to, in fact, throughout life. 'Progression', 'achievement' – as we saw in relation to adult life – can bring their own problems. But by contrast, the hopes and expectations of most women centre on marriage and children, and therefore relate essentially to young adulthood. The years after marriage are virtually unscripted. The romantic idyll, with all its myriad permutations in songs, films, stories or advertisements, typically ends with the uniting of the man and woman, whose 'happily ever after' is not documented. For many married women, this probably imposes an additional sense of loneliness in a life which may already be felt as isolated. Attempts at further development, on one's own part, during later life, may be a lonely venture and are likely to demand a good deal of courage. Marriage, for women, also means, in important ways, a new identity. The change of name is itself symbolic of other changes in which the husband's role in life, his purposes, his needs, will be expected to take precedence over those of his wife.

The fact that women's traditional goals are those of marriage and family, while those of men traditionally relate to the wider world is, of course, far from accidental; it arises out of the whole relation which defines our notion of gender. It can be seen at many levels. Not only do most girls live in eager, intense anticipation of romantic love, followed by the personal fulfilment of family life, while most boys are scornfully dismissing such preoccupations – or at most, conceding that marriage and children may play a small part in their own future lives. The same assumptions underlie the very different attitudes that we take towards the *unmarried*, according to their sex. Where bachelors are involved, we see them as light-hearted – fancy-free – if a little selfish, a little irresponsible. With spinsters, the image is quite different. Above all, they are seen as pitiable. 'But she's quite attractive!' we exclaim with surprise. The inescapable implication is that no one asked her; unlike the bachelor, who chose not to marry, the poor woman never got the chance.

There is something of a paradox in this differential definition of the life goals of males and females. From the available statistics, it seems that it is men, rather than women, who have the greater need to be married. Men are more likely, if they are unmarried rather than married, to die early, have poor health, resort to crime or succumb to alcoholism or breakdown. For women, the situation is the other way round. Perhaps this should make us reflect on the arbitrary nature of our sex-role stereotypes. If we can accept that men have feelings too, that, like women, they need the affection, the support, the intimacy of other human beings, then perhaps we shall begin to break through the prison of our conventional masculine and feminine roles, which, in governing their life careers, diminish boys and girls, men and women alike. We can hope, at least, to move beyond the man witnessed by Stevi Jackson who, refusing a kiss from his two-year-old son, told him, 'You're too old for that now – it's not manly.'

9 EMBODIED LIVING

Looking in the mirror one morning, you notice a few grey hairs around the temples. Suddenly, you see that you are middle-aged. Tiny bodily changes can, sometimes, usher in a startling sense of personal progression, define a new stage in our journey through time. From early life to late, the bodies we inhabit go through their own dramatic transformations. In shape, in strength, in function, our physical selves as babies are strikingly unlike those we will have as teenagers, or again as old people. How should we view this physical progression? Do we, as persons, grow as our bodies grow, decline as they decline? Or is the spirit's journey of another order altogether – a journey with its own, different milestones, shifts, transitions?

To this basic question, different people would answer differently. Some individuals live in close communion with their bodies. They give careful attention to their own physical functioning, accord great personal significance to bodily changes. For such people, their own embodiments are not merely the vehicles which they happen to occupy; they make up the very stuff of personal experience. In this perspective, bodily changes entail personal transitions; the physical phases which people undergo represent the basic, the essential stages of their psychological development as they go through life. People who see things in this way are likely to take a broadly conventional view as to the overall shape of the life cycle. For them, the peak of life is young adulthood, when physical powers are at their height. Conversely, they view old age – when the body grows frail and vulnerable – as the period of inevitable personal decline. There are other people who see things differently. For those people, the logic of the body, the changes which it undergoes, are experienced as independent of psychological life and personal development. As with the vicissitudes of the weather, accommodation must be made to the varying limits set, at different life periods, by one's own physique. Yet physical functions do not define personal ones, and, as human beings, our progression is not contained within the changing phases of our physical embodiment.

It is generally expected that women and men will have rather different experiences of their changing embodiments. Women, so we tend to believe, are much more subject, psychologically, to transition, because of the changing rhythms of their bodies. According to the usual stereotype, it is the monthly menstrual cycle which significantly regulates emotion, attitude and capacity. Men, by contrast, we believe, respond to events in ways that are uninfluenced by such physical rhythms. If we see women as dominated, within each monthly cycle, by the regular biological changes which they undergo, we also see the larger pattern of their lives as shaped by their biology. Whereas we expect that men will sustain their sexual vitality into old age, we set a definite limit, in the menopause, to that of women. And because, as women are usually defined, sexual and reproductive functioning is seen as central to female personhood, this limit, for women, carries implications of major personal loss, perhaps even the ending of their lives as women.

In the way that, as individuals, we experience our physical selves, there is probably much more diversity, for women and for men, than the stereotype would have it. Some women do feel themselves, as persons, to fluctuate with their periods; but other women do not find their experience to be like this. While sometimes the menopause brings in the major personal changes we associate with it, this is not always so. And conversely, there are men for whom the experience of changes in physical structure or function seems to carry the largest personal implications – to define an expansion or a contraction in the continuing development of one's self.

Yet if people vary in the meaning they attribute to their own embodiments, there are surely phases, for all of us, during which our physical selves assume greater or lesser salience. For certain stretches in our lives, our bodies may be like the old clothes we generally wear – familiar, comfortable, taken for granted. But at other times, they demand the closest, the most intense, the most urgent attention. For most people, this happens, above all, during adolescence. Then, many aspects of our physical selves undergo change. The body comes to function differently, with a new voice register, or the advent of menstruation. Physical shape changes, with altered bodily proportions. And surfaces develop their own long-term or temporary changes, in the growth of body hair, or the outbreak of spotty skin.

The intense concern with which individuals experience the physical changes of puberty arises, perhaps, out of the sense that these changes essentially govern the odds that, as an adult, one will carry. Arbitrary though they are, none of us can escape the barrage of messages, in our society, as to how an attractive man, and – still more – an attractive woman, *should* look. In these terms, most people inevitably find themselves wanting. And this is likely to entail the experience of failing to become a proper adult. Since we tend to think that 'good looks', particularly for women, are, during adult life, the key to personal desirability and personal choice, not looking 'right' in early adulthood may be equated with poor life chances.

Sexual attractiveness is a dimension which is given differential significance according to gender. Whereas we often judge men in other terms, it is rare for women, of whatever age, to be evaluated without some reference to this dimension. For most women in our society, their own physical attractiveness is probably a life-long preoccupation. And this preoccupation carries with it a dread of age, since, for women, to be attractive is to be youthful. Young women, therefore, represent in some sense the standard to which older women aspire – yet which they can never achieve. Try as we will, through skilful choice of clothing, careful management of hair and face, we cannot entirely hide the bodily effects of time. At fifty, we cannot ultimately succeed in looking twenty. Women who are genuinely young – who achieve without effort their smooth skin, firm breasts, clean jaw, luxuriant hair, ease of movement – such women can arouse complicated feelings in women who are middle-aged. There goes a young woman, looking as one would love to look oneself. Yet she is dissatisfied with her physical self, even seems unaware of how attractive, how enviable, she is. Youth, one may murmur bitterly, is truly wasted on the young.

This perspective on our physical embodiments contains within it a sense of time as the ultimate threat. It is a perspective which views our bodily selves as personal packaging – packaging which assumes its greatest significance in early adulthood, and thereafter gets more and more spoiled. Not only does this view carry the sense of age as personally catastrophic, at least for women. It also incorporates an essential disrespect for the particularity, the distinctiveness, of individual embodiments. If we see our physical selves as merely versions of a generalized ideal, then we can only try, as best we may, to mould, adorn, present them to approximate the standard pattern. The expression we give them is not their own – it is something to be imposed on them. Their own character, such as it is, may seem quite contrary to what we would like to make it. To this extent, we experience our bodies – especially as they age – as recalcitrant objects which must be coerced, resisted, fought against.

Is it possible to take another perspective, to see our physical embodiments in other terms? Can we adopt a view which accords significance and value to the particular bodies we inhabit – a value which is not diminished by the changes which they undergo as the years progress? In thinking about this, we should, perhaps, reflect on the way in which, in our relations with others, we actually experience each other as embodied persons.

As the conventional wisdom has it, in our encounters with others, we are affected by particular aspects of their physique. If the man with whom, as a woman, you are talking has the 'right' sort of physical masculinity, then he will more easily be able to influence you, to turn things to his own advantage. And perhaps, if this is someone you have just met, you may have made an instantaneous, hardly conscious comparison of your new acquaintance with the stereotyped masculine ideal. But, as things progress, this feature of your attention will probably have been entirely replaced by other sorts of awareness. Our dealings with each other are based on the subtle and delicate readings of body language. And the currency of this language is not one which can be reduced to the physical features whose significance we usually emphasize. The modes through which we intuitively communicate with each other are not a matter of physical size, muscularity, proportion. Body language is constituted by tiny, often barely perceptible changes in bodily posture, gesture, movement, voice; it is essentially a question of how we use our bodies.

If we consider our social interactions in these terms, it is obvious that body language often carries messages that are at variance with explicit, deliberate ones. Something indefinable in the expression of the eyes conveys the inner emptiness of the welcome offered. Or the confidence of the walk, the facial expression, is somehow betrayed by the little tremor in the voice, the slight stiffness of the jaw. The discrepancies between deliberate self-presentation on the one hand, and communications inadvertently made through subtle bodily cues on the other – these discrepancies are a central theme in the work of Erving Goffman, mentioned in the previous chapter. As Goffman puts it, the 'signs given' by conscious and intentional communications, are often contradicted by 'signs given off' – the involuntary physical expression of our real feelings. In this way, our wish to express certain attitudes, even to present ourselves as a certain kind of person, may be undermined by the physical expressiveness which we cannot control.*

Not only does the body have its own rich language of communication – a language in which we are all well versed. Each person's embodiment represents a unique linguistic source – is a unique speaker of the language. Fundamentally, the way we hold ourselves, the way we physically move, conveys, carries, bespeaks our own particular ways of reacting, of feeling – it tells how we position ourselves towards our lives. Bodily stance is, perhaps, the very clearest expression of our personhood. If we

* Goffman, E., *The Presentation of Self in Everyday Life*, Doubleday, 1959.

look at things like this, human embodiment takes on a quite different character from the one we usually give it. In our thinking about our physical selves, it is the objective aspects of bodies which we generally emphasize. Height and breadth, size of breasts, hips, shoulders or waist, facial proportions, hair colour, smoothness of skin – these are the features which make up the 'desirable' or 'undesirable' packaging of the self. Yet, paradoxically, these things are likely to be salient only when we distance ourselves from people, as people. Once we begin to experience each other as human beings, somehow these features melt away. In conjuring up the image of an intimate friend you find, to your amazement, that you cannot remember the colour of his eyes. In years of responding to his unique bodily expressiveness, in seeing him as a person rather than as an object, you have forgotten to notice the surface details which seem wholly irrelevant to your experience of him.

It is, perhaps, through an insistent attention to the objective aspects of people's embodiments that we often act to deny their humanity. Racist or sexist attitudes are given expression in the refusal to recognize the person within the black skin, the female body. Within this perspective, individual human beings are grossly diminished – reduced to the typification of a social category. It is an experience all too familiar to those with a physical disability. The lack of muscular control, for instance, which afflicts people suffering cerebral palsy, does not eliminate their distinctive personhood. Nor does it obscure the richness, the uniqueness, of their bodily expressiveness – a language which, like that of the rest of us, can only be learned through a sustained, attentive responsiveness to that particular person. Such a response, though, seems rarely to be given to those with disabilities. Here is Sue, speaking as a victim of multiple sclerosis:

> Disability can and sometimes does interfere with the practical running of a life, but it is the reaction and non-action of society which causes disablement. There

is no such thing as THE DISABLED, there are just people.*

If women, ethnic minorities and those with disabilities tend to suffer such 'objectification', this is also very often the case for elderly people. Because our habitual view of human embodiment is that of personal packaging, it carries an automatic devaluation of physical ageing. For many people, the sight of an old woman is the sight of wrinkled skin, faltering movements, shaky voice and hands. As a human being, it seems, she amounts to no more than this, and, as such, is viewed with repugnance. Seen in this way, not merely by strangers, but often even by those who daily care for them, it is no wonder that elderly people themselves can come to feel a painful sense of alienation from their own physical embodiments. Yet how differently that elderly woman is experienced if we happen to love her! Like a sweet song clearly heard through the interference of a radio set, her bodily expressiveness continues, as it has always done, to convey the altogether special qualities of her human particularity. In that familiar crooked smile, that little lift of the head, that touch of the hand, that expression in the eyes, that inflection of the voice – in all this, you seem to be in the closest, the most immediate contact with a unique and beloved human spirit.

Our usual view of human embodiment contains an implicit rejection of physical ageing. To see our bodily selves in terms of their own unique personal language offers a different perspective, in which there is continuity, and, in the midst of physical ageing, we nevertheless retain what is essentially significant in human terms. If this perspective makes old age look rather different, we should also see how earlier life phases appear within its view.

When we think of the significance of the body for children growing up, it is typically in terms of the personal packaging image. Though the final embodiment will not be clearly estab-

* Campling, J. (ed.), *Images of Ourselves: Women with Disabilities Talking*, Routledge & Kegan Paul, 1981.

lished until after puberty, it is to signs of the stereotyped image of masculine or feminine physique that we usually attend. Indications of strength, size, muscularity will, we think, stand the boy in good stead, while girls are doing well if they seem to be developing pretty faces and dainty, curvaceous bodies. All this, perhaps, is the way we think about development in the abstract; it represents our generalized psychology. When we actually encounter children, when we are personally engaged with them, things may be very different. This is because children themselves usually have a body language which is particularly striking and vivid – which itself compels our attention. In their moment-to-moment living, the young seem somehow not to experience the same constraints, the same inhibitions, which are so often conveyed in the bearing, the carriage, the movements of adult people. This gives the physical expressiveness of most children much greater mobility and freedom than we usually see in men and women. There is also, generally, less ambiguity, more transparency, in youthful body language. Whereas what is expressed in adults' embodiments is often obscure or contradictory, the expressiveness of children is typically much clearer, more open, more all-of-a-piece. 'Signs given' tend to accord with 'signs given off'.

How is it that people come to lose the vividness, fluidity, naturalness of their childhood embodiments? Surely the process must start in adolescence, when most of us acquire our anxious sense of physical inadequacy, our realization that our bodies fall far short of the ideal size, shape, surface? Or that the 'attractive' physique with which we have been blessed has only a few years to go before the ravages of time will remove our temporary advantage? Defining ourselves in this way must inevitably mean an inhibition, a rejection, in some sense, of our spontaneous physical expressiveness. And in this, not only do we generally acquire, in adulthood, a kind of physical constraint; we also, perhaps, often come to feel a sense of dissociation, even alienation, from our embodiments.

To feel separated, alienated, from your own body means being cut off, out of touch, with what it may be expressing.

Paradoxically, for most men and women, it is others who have greater access to the clues of our body language than we do ourselves. They may catch glimpses of our real feelings, sense where we really stand, see things of which we ourselves remain unaware. The experience of seeing ourselves in action, on someone's home movie, or of hearing our own tape-recorded voice, is usually little short of traumatic. This is not just because the expression of our physical selves seems strange and unfamiliar. Beyond the strangeness, there is often a sense of acute embarrassment, even repugnance. It is as if our own person, when directly encountered in this way, is someone we cannot really like, would rather disown.

Lack of contact with the direct, intimate expression of our selves is, perhaps, personally costly. In some sense, it means that our own experience is alien to us, that we are not intuitively in touch with the personal stance we are adopting towards our lives. If this is so, then we cannot know the meaning of the journey we are making, cannot see what it is that we have sustained through our lives so far, or to what we are now looking. Nor is it possible to reflect upon the personal positions we habitually take, and, perhaps, to find we need to alter them. It may be that, through our self-imposed alienation from our physical selves – through our obsessive and anxious concern with the inadequacies of our physique – we come to live our lives more blindly than we need.

In our own society, judgments such as these seem strange. Yet they accord with the experience of people who try, in one way or another, to enlarge their awareness of their own physical selves. Whether through massage, the Alexander method, or the techniques of biofeedback, the exploration of one's own embodiment brings with it unexpected and remarkable discoveries about one's own personal feelings, personal reactions. In noticing how your shoulders, through what seems to be their own volition, habitually position themselves in a particular way – a way which is obstinately resistant to your attempts to hold them differently – you begin to glimpse something of your own intimate experience. The way you hold your shoulders seems to have to do with a profound resolution, on your part, to stay in charge of things, to avoid, at all costs, acknowledging weakness and vulnerability. You notice that their position seems particularly rigid and fixed in situations where you are under stress, where it is specially difficult to maintain your sense of being in control.

When people begin, through methods such as these, to realize more about aspects of their own personal stance, it becomes possible to dwell upon them, to mull them over, to reflect on what they mean. Sometimes, this can involve change. You learn, through biofeedback, to control your blood pressure, and by doing so, to reduce your level of personal tension. By focusing upon your own physical expressiveness, by listening sensitively to your own body language, somehow you have come to gain access to your own experience, to achieve a greater grasp of your own life. In this, you have acquired a kind of personal freedom, through which you are, potentially, less imprisoned by the shackles of habitual reactions.

To understand our human lives – the continuities and the developments of which we are capable – we need, it seems, to approach our bodies with respect, and with imagination. As long as we see them only in terms of their objective features, we shall continue to view age and time as personally catastrophic. In our selves, as adults, we shall remain physically constrained, and out of touch with much in our own experience. Only if we can recognize, in our expressions of our embodiments, the profound, subtle, delicate language of the human spirit, shall we be able to accord proper recognition, proper value, to every human body.

10 THE FAMILY CONTEXT

When people write their autobiographies – their account of their personal journey through time – they seldom begin with their own birth, or their own earliest memories. Instead, they start the story with the circumstances and events of their parents', or even their grandparents', lives. Somehow these lives, which were lived without their own engagement, their own presence, and which may involve people who never even knew them, are felt to *belong* to the person who is their descendant. It is as though that person's life, identity, and place in the world is in part defined by the family members who have gone before.

In the huge significance accorded to the family by our ordinary understanding it seems that time represents a major dimension of meaning. From what we know of human history, the family has, in most societies, entailed two central social functions: lineage, and inheritance. It is through our family lineage that we come to have the *name* by which we are identified. This identification is, of course, different for men and for women, since it is the woman who, on marrying, takes the name of her husband, and it is his name which is given to the children they have. This is, of course, one facet of gender differentiation. But in any case, the name that people carry has a human significance with many connotations. As bearers of particular names, we are all, in some sense, carrying 'the line' forward – adding our own life on to a line of lives which reaches back through past generations, and which may stretch out forward, too, through a succession of lives yet to be lived. This way of seeing one's life is obviously more profoundly meaningful to some people than to others. Some individuals personally research their family ancestry, or construct detailed and elaborate family trees. For such people, their membership, their place, in an intricate historical family process must provide a rich dimension of meaning in their sense of personal identity. A similarly deep significance in lineage must underlie the grieving of others when their family 'line' dies out, because no children are born to the latest generation in the family.

Families give their children an 'inheritance' as well as a name. In our own society, this function has historically had a male bias, like that of lineage, and perhaps this is still quite often the case. In economic terms, the young generation inherits the parental 'estate': its riches, its responsibilities, its privileges – or merely its debts, perhaps. But psychologically, family inheritance has a much wider meaning than this. In some sense, all children are given the heritage of their family's, and especially their parents', lives: just by being the children of that family, they *inherit* their parents' experience and situation in life. There is also another kind of family inheritance in which many people believe: that of heredity. The kinds of people we become, the courses of the lives we lead, are, I would myself argue, not the product of our genetic make-up. Nevertheless, there are individuals who do see their lives in these terms, and who believe themselves to be defined by a particular pattern of gifts and liabilities – one version of a general pattern which is characteristic of all their family members. For people like this, their family membership is central in governing their own particular life career. Even for those who do not attribute this kind of function to human heredity, the physical resemblances which our genes do un-doubtedly carry can give a peculiar poignancy to family ancestry. You see, in an old family photograph, a previously unknown great-aunt whose face looks so exactly your sister's – the same short upper lip, the same tilt of the nose, the same expression in the eyes – and suddenly a past life becomes part of your own present, and your own experience is somehow momentarily united with that of long-gone ancestors.

Being born a member of a family means being guaranteed, by the mere fact of physical existence, some place in the human world. To belong to a family is to possess, automatically, a particular social significance. In a fundamental way, it is our family membership which gives us solidity as human beings encountering the world. From this point of view, it is not surprising, perhaps, that family *dis*inheritance – being cut off, *disowned* by one's family – has been seen as the ultimate, the most terrible, human sanction. Nor does it seem puzzling that nearly every person who comes to know of their own adoption experiences a vital, an urgent personal need to find out who his or her real parents are. In explaining why this is a personal necessity, such people typically speak of the knowledge of their biological parentage, and biological family membership, as enabling them to know what kind of people they really are.

Our status as members of families may be more or less important to us at different times in our lives, and may mean very different things at those times. During their adolescence, many people are concerned to reject this aspect as defining themselves or their lives in any important way. There is a sense of protest against being viewed as one's father's son, the daughter of such-and-such a family, or someone's younger sister. Some young people engage in fantasies of having *real* parents elsewhere – parents who are quite different from the ones they are living with. Or sometimes, a young person struggles against the very idea of being anything other than themselves: like the crab imagined by William James, they indignantly insist, 'I am myself, myself alone.' Underlying these attitudes, there is perhaps a personally vital resistance against a kind of human diminution. Families offer their members a share in a human identity whose breadth and solidity stems from its reach across the generations, and across many different kinds of life. But conversely, such an identity may represent a prison. Unless each new family member can establish for themselves a new, unique, personally created life course, they are condemned to live out merely one version of a script already written – a script from the family repertoire of plays and characters. Here is Ronald Laing's account of this kind of situation as it applies to one particular family:

We can just glimpse in this family a drama perpetuated

over three generations – the players are two women and a man: first, mother, daughter and father; second, mother, daughter and daughter's son. Daughter's father dies – daughter conceives a son to replace her father. The play's the thing. The actors come and go. As they die, others are born. The new born enters the part vacated by the newly dead. The system perpetuates itself over generations; the young are introduced to the parts that the dead once played.

David is playing the part his grandfather once played. What will happen when he gets married? Marry his grandmother, produce his mother in his daughter, who will marry his father and produce him in his grandson?*

If we think of the significance of the family context, in personal development, it is clear that living in one's family entails being powerfully characterized. No other human context so strongly marks out, defines and recognizes the particular individual identity of its members; the family is a place where it is impossible to be anonymous – just one of a crowd. The enormous power of family characterizations must partly derive from the role that time plays in them. From the very moment of birth, a new family member is viewed as showing particular tendencies, particular ways of reacting, a particular personhood. The little movements of tiny babies, their slight changes of expression, their way of crying or not crying, seem to convey highly significant directions in their personality; in them, parents see momentous clues as to the kind of person their baby already is, and will continue to be. As the baby grows older her behaviour, her reactions, are seen to confirm these expectations in all sorts of ways. For children growing up in their families, ascriptions like these are not merely interpretations imposed on them; they actually constitute in a basic sense what is felt to be their real identity. In this, continuity over time must add to the feeling of

* Laing, R. D., 'Intervention in social situations', in Walrond-Skinner, S. (ed.), *Developments in Family Therapy*, Routledge & Kegan Paul, 1981.

validity. Aged eight, you are all the more sure that you are a stubborn, determined sort of person, because that is how you have always been known, and how you have always known yourself, for as long as you can remember. And even before that, as a baby, it seems you would not be quieted, you stubbornly refused to settle, until you had got what you wanted.

Nor is time the only dimension which gives solidity to this kind of characterization. The reach of that identity extends beyond the literal confines of the household. We live out our family selves, in innumerable ways, in our encounters with parents, sisters, brothers, in-laws, uncles, nieces, or grandparents. But we also come to define our wider engagements in terms of that same identity. This is because families act not merely as sounding boards for their members, but in a sense, as co-producers. On his first day at secondary school, a boy gets into a fight. Hearing about this, his family, who *know* him to be a fair person, *realize* that the other boy must have picked on him; and it is in the light of this interpretation that they all discuss how he should act the next time this happens. To at least some extent, we all bring our experiences, our expectations – the hopes, struggles, difficulties of our extra-familial lives – to the audience of our families. It is the concern, the interest, even the investment, of our family intimates in how we conduct our daily lives outside home, that ensures the extension, the continuity of our family character.

The identity we acquire as children through growing up in families is surely a very basic one. When, in middle age, people visit their parents, they may find that they are talking and reacting like the children they were: they actually feel, perhaps with dismay, that they have reverted to being their mother's child again. Or a man, known to all his friends as a generous, large-spirited, compassionate person, suddenly becomes envious, spiteful, petty when he meets a brother who was his rival during childhood. If our childish family identities endure so long in our lives, this is not really surprising. The family context is one in which the participants have for each other a supreme importance. Whereas in many other life contexts, one's presence as a particular kind of person may be more or less immaterial, in families one's own particular personhood is very significant – it matters vitally. One way of reflecting on this is to consider the situation of children who grow up in children's homes, without their own families. What such children miss most of all, it seems, is the *partiality* of family feeling. Paradoxically, the impersonal benevolence of well run homes may constitute the opposite of what is longed for; it is passionate relationships that children crave, not impartial kindness. Even where parents act cruelly and brutally towards their children, this in no way lessens their immense personal significance for the children themselves – as I saw for myself while working in an approved school for delinquent boys.

Though childish family identity exerts such power and endures so long, nevertheless many people make determined efforts to escape it. This is particularly true of many adolescents, who may see breaking out of their family character as the only way of establishing their adulthood. But to do this is always very difficult. A new hair-style, a new way of talking, the abandoning of previous interests or plans for oneself, the taking up with a new group of friends – all these may produce a profound resistance from parents, or brothers and sisters. 'But that's not like you!' may be the indignant, resentful reaction. New projects may be contemptuously dismissed as 'just a phase she's going through'. Even slight shifts in direction can arouse angry reactions which seem out of all proportion to what they entail.

Because family life involves a network of close personal relationships, family identities are essentially intertwined. If the attempted shifts in position of one member arouse, as they do, a sense of anxiety, disturbance, anger in other members, this has to do with the multiple and intimate ways in which one person's movement necessarily calls for movement in others. Family life has been called a 'dance'; and this metaphor expresses the interlinking of lives that families involve. We all think, feel, act, not in isolation, but *towards* others, who we expect to think, feel and act in ways that we can more or less anticipate. It is only through the position of others that one's own position has meaning. The son's 'mechanical flair' takes its particular meaning, in that family, from the practical ineptness, the lack of interest in mechanical things, of both his mother and his sister – in contrast to his highly skilled, practical father, a qualified motor mechanic and a competent handyman around the house. The older sister's 'kindness', her 'gentleness' – entailed in her future direction as a children's nurse – is given its daily reality by her helpfulness toward her 'vulnerable' younger brother who, as everyone can see, is so clearly 'dependent' on her. If that younger brother begins to assert himself, to act in independent ways, to rebel against his sister's protectiveness, then her own family identity is undermined.

In considering its impact on personal development, we tend to think of family life as something rather static. The cereal-packet image represents an extreme example: the prototypical mother, father, son and daughter who, regardless of their particular age, merely mark a moment in an enduring family unit which has lasted in much the same form since the children were born, and will not alter its basic character until they leave home. This is probably very unlike the experience of any single family. Family life necessarily involves changes for its members. Families experience both arrivals and departures – each calling for an alteration in the dance. New steps must be added, to allow for the performance of a new member. If the dance is not to lose its rhythm completely, somehow changes must be made which compensate for the departure of one of the dancers. In households which break up, which suffer the death, the desertion, the absence of a member, in family units which change their composition frequently or drastically – in any of these circumstances, prolonged and difficult effort is called for, so that the dance can be sustained. Nor do family dances encompass only those who are physically present in the household. After divorce, for instance, the absent father may continue to hold a critical part in things; the subject of the mother's constant angry and bitter preoccupation, of the daughter's passionate loyalty and longing, he remains a partner towards whom they dance.

Family changes may be momentous for our future lives. And

it is not only physical changes in family composition which demand adjustments from the members. The upheavals of family life which can occur when children reach their teens, derive from the fact that if adolescents are to develop as persons, then others in the family, particularly parents, must change too. And even apart from adolescence, in most families quite radical changes probably do take place in the delicately balanced network of reciprocal relationships which make up their particular dance. A girl who has always found her older sister bossy, domineering, unsympathetic, discovers to her delight that, after all, they share many of the same feelings, the same hopes, the same anxieties; and their relationship begins to take on an altogether different character. Or a son, who had previously always been on his father's side in the continual parental quarrels, finds himself beginning to see things differently. It seems to him that it is his mother's position that he can understand, sympathize with; and it is this position with which he now aligns himself.

We generally regard the family's developmental significance as benign. Yet the personal intensity of family contexts entails, potentially, great suffering. Families, after all, are the arena in which many children (as well as many wives) are physically or sexually assaulted. Such abuse has been the subject of a number of psychologists working in New Hampshire, U.S.A.* As one of them, Murray Strauss, has remarked, it is in their families, where most people expect to receive the greatest love, the greatest trust, the greatest support, that children can experience the greatest personal violence, the greatest physical terror they will ever know. Like other researchers, this team has concluded that parental abuse of children is very widespread, with publicly reported cases representing merely the tip of the iceberg.

How should we view all this? How does it happen that, in so many instances, people can grow up to be adults who terrorize their small children? In thinking about this, it seems important to

---

* Finkelhor, D. *et al.* (eds.), *The Dark Side of Families*, Sage Publications, 1983.

notice that parents who beat up their children are usually men. And such fathers seldom actually hate or reject the children they abuse in this way. On the contrary they – and often their wives – see it as perfectly consistent with the normal paternal role to engage in periodic physical violence towards their children, even if they are likely to concede that sometimes they go too far. If physical assault is seen, in the context of the families where it happens, as generally understandable and normal behaviour on the part of fathers, this is less likely to be the case where sexual abuse is concerned. Nevertheless, as another member of this team, David Finkelhor, argues, sexually assaulting children is, like physically battering them, merely an extension of the conventional masculine role. Men are *expected*, in our society, to select younger, smaller, less experienced sexual partners. Male sexuality is *expected* to be divorced from affection, to be a matter of domination and conquest. To force sexual relations on a small, terrified daughter is, therefore, merely to play out, in an extreme form, the prototypical masculine predator. In these terms, the physical or sexual abuse of children which is quite a common phenomenon in families arises essentially out of socially sanctioned gender roles. Men who engage in this kind of behaviour are, perhaps, only living out extreme versions of the machismo part which, from childhood on, they have been expected to play.

When we think of how the family affects its members, it is children that we usually have in mind. But families have their impact on adults, too. Children, it has been said, make of men and women fathers and mothers – a status, identity, role in life which have huge significance. One aspect of parenthood is its differential meaning for men and women, and this in turn acts to alter the relationship between husband and wife. Being a parent, particularly being a mother, also carries certain implications to do with personal change, and personal stability. In general, while we expect and encourage the young to change, we do not anticipate that their mothers will similarly develop. This can often mean that women are expected to act merely as a static backdrop to their children's development, and that new directions, ostensibly open, are in effect barred to them. For many mothers in this situation, the departure of the children for whom they have acted in this way can entail, beyond simple loss, even a sense of personal betrayal.

In the life of families, time has many resonances. Other human institutions segregate their members by the age they are. Only adults may work, only children may go to school. In practice, people tend to choose their associates from much narrower age-bands than these. Anyone over twenty-five would probably feel extremely uncomfortable at a disco. Middle-aged people choose, if they can, jobs where they will be among those of similar age; while a young person will go for places with plenty of young workmates. But families, by definition, mix the ages of their members; in families at least two generations, perhaps three, live intimately together. Because of this chronological mix, family members can, indeed necessarily must, in some sense partake of the lives of others who are at different points in the life cycle. Through her close relationship with her grandmother, a little girl comes to know, to possess for herself something of her grandmother's very different childhood, and her present experience. By witnessing the new baby, seeing what he is like and how he changes, she acquires within herself something of what it means to be very young. Many of the things that children experience in their families have to do with their own futures. They learn first-hand and intimately about the adult lives of men and women; and this covers what they will *not* be, just as much as it conveys what they probably will become. And if fathers, for their small sons, represent a possible future prospect, the converse is equally true. Many parents find their own childhood recapitulated in that of their children, and see their childish lives again lived out in the person of their son or daughter. One of the strands underlying this sense of continuity across time must be the fact of physical resemblance. Just as mother and daughter, leafing through an old family album, see with delighted amazement, that the mother looked, at age ten, just like her eleven-year-old daughter looks now – so children can sometimes, with pleasure or dismay, see their future adult selves physically represented in their parents.

In families, then, concern with time past is intimately inter-woven with time which is yet to come. As parents, men and women are necessarily concerned with their children's future, encompassing even the stage at which they themselves will have died. And this means that current life – its choices, its directions, its disappointments – is constantly viewed in terms of the signifi-cance it holds for the future, perhaps the quite distant future. In this concern, large spans of time may be incorporated. A grand-father who urges his grandson to save money, sadly reflects on the different course his own life might have taken if only he had had the means to supplement his parents' meagre contribution to his education.

Time is, of course, part of the currency in much family conversation. It is through a temporal perspective that young family members are habitually viewed. The rate at which a baby is developing is perhaps a universal preoccupation – how already he can say Mama and Dada, how late she is in crawling, compared with her sister. The acquisition of new skills, the development of new interests, the growing understanding and responsiveness of children as they become older, represent for parents the major source of concern, pride, or anxiety. It is to such changes that visitors are expected to attend; and judgments that children are changing, developing, are satisfying not just to parents, but to children themselves. Most children are, in fact, much preoccupied with the changes that come with time. Not only is there a close comparison of relative skills and competen-cies, in relation to age; age is also assumed to be a valid basis for differential treatment. This means that the older-ness or younger-ness of sisters and brothers – with all its implications of competence, rights, privileges – represents a major axis in the relationship between them.

Most people also experience, in the intimacy of their family relationships, a shared rehearsing of the passing of family time. The early years of life, that change so fast, that are so fleeting – for parents these are generally felt to be precious. Even if there are no photographs to be displayed, memories of what children were like as babies will be lovingly recalled, as will the funny or touching sayings of young children, their striking or poignant early encounters with the world. Though the often repeated anecdote may produce only an embarrassed grimace from the child himself, nevertheless such rehearsals carry a sense of continuity in personal identity. The dramas, the patterning, the historical shape of family life are also carried in the shared recollections of family members. After many years apart, a middle-aged brother and sister meet at a family wedding. Their reminiscences about childhood may give each a sense of vital personal confirmation, personal recognition. Or perhaps, on the contrary, they open up a chasm. To her dismay, the woman finds her brother does not remember at all, or else remember things in terms that are unbelievably different from her own. Our childish family identity is one which, perhaps, we never lose; and this gives to those who know it – with whom it is lodged – great power in confirming or undermining our sense of ourselves.

11 LOSS AND ENDING

'Don't ever change – please stay just the way you are!' So, perhaps, lovers have always begged each other. But this is a promise that can never be kept. To live in time is – in every sense – to *suffer change*. Paradoxically, it is just when life is at its fullest, its richest, its most joyous, that we are often most keenly aware of its transience. As poets, throughout the ages, remind us, all that is precious, all that is lovely, will pass from us; there is, in Hopkins' words, no braid or brace to keep back beauty from vanishing away. However tightly we clasp our beloved to us, the embrace cannot survive death. And our own inevitable death will rob us so soon of everything.

What part do loss and ending play in our understanding of living in time? When we think of human loss, it is usually such life events as bereavement, redundancy, being deserted, or having a miscarriage which come most readily to mind. Because of this, we are apt to think of loss as something which affects adults rather than children. But, from earliest childhood on, human life involves the experience of change, loss, ending. However carefully children may be held back from contact with people who are terminally ill, death cannot be kept from breaking through. The beloved cat which is run over, the wounded bird which could not live, for all the care lavished upon it – for even the youngest children there is no protection against the pain and grief of such personal losses. Nor can children be spared more human kinds of loss. Childhood entails being subject to changes in relationship that are consequent upon the decisions of adults. Because adults come and go in ways that children cannot control, being young perhaps always involves suffering certain painful departures and separations from those one loves. And children, like adults, know changes in their lives – changes of which, however, they are less often in charge, and may meet with inward protest. To leave all your friends because of having to change school, to abandon, when the family moves house, the intimate familiarity of your bedroom, the secret places in the garden you know so well – these changes can produce real grieving, genuine mourning. And this is so even where the new school seems an exciting prospect, or the new house and neighbourhood represent entry to a larger world, of greater personal possibilities.

In human life, every change, every new departure, is in some sense a loss. However much we have longed for this marriage, this promotion, this kind of work, the birth of this baby – when it comes, it also brings for us an ending of other things. This means that even the happiest events in our lives cast their own kind of shadow. Sometimes, that shadow is strangely, unexpectedly dark. The psychiatrist Richard Rahe, who made a study of the personal impact of different life events,* found that the most positive changes can often be experienced as actually traumatic. Men and women whom fortune seems to bless, who are granted what they have long sought after and struggled for – such people can often react with tension, stress, illness, just as though they had failed, rather than succeeded, in achieving these desirable goals. This seems to be because, whether good or bad, major changes in our lives demand a great deal of accommodation. We have to shift our position, to enter into new territory, and in doing so, to leave behind us for ever what was known, familiar ground. In a sense, when we make any large-scale changes, we have to say goodbye to our earlier selves. The stag party of the bridegroom, on the eve of his wedding, represents a ritual expression of mourning for his never-to-be-recovered bachelor days. And behind the paradoxical sense of sadness we feel amidst our elation at the new-found freedoms of our teenage years, lies a grieving for the childhood we have lost. It is this loss of our own selves which is the theme of Hopkins's poem 'Margaret':

* Rahe, R. H., 'Life crisis and health change', in May, P.R.A. and Winterborn, J.R. (eds.), *Psychotropic Drug Response: Prediction Studies*, G.C. Thomas, 1969.

Margaret, are you grieving
Over Goldengrove unleaving?
Trees, like the things of man, you
With your fresh thoughts care for, can you?
Ah, as the heart grows older
It will come to such sights colder
By and by, nor spare a sigh
Though worlds of wanwood leafmeal lie.

Hopkins's theme is the loss of sensibility that the passage of time can bring to human beings. This theme seems, for many people, to resonate with their own experience. Poetry and literature are full of such echoes. And in particular, it is the 'glory and the freshness' with which Wordsworth saw childhood endowed which many men and women mourn. Wistfully, many adults gaze back at their earlier lives, when the seasons were so varied and so vivid, when the scent of everything was so strong, when joy and pain were so keenly, poignantly felt. As their bodies have thickened, their youthful slenderness and suppleness gone, so, people can feel, their spirit too has grown coarser, harder, more callous. They do not really seem to feel things any more. Perhaps the meaning of this experience has to do with the lack of adequate kinds of mourning for the changes which have taken place. If this is so, we should reflect on how it is that, in their further living, some people are able to survive, even to be strengthened, by major kinds of loss, while others are personally devastated by them.

In both our general understanding and our official psychology about personal development, we place the very greatest weight on one particular loss – the loss of a mother in early childhood. For many years, it was officially pronounced that the damage consequent on such losses was personally devastating, and irreversible. During the last fifteen years, however, a large number of children have been carefully studied, following the death or desertion or absence of their mother while they were still young. The dire predictions have not generally been borne out. Where children have been personally damaged, this seems to have been the outcome of the marital friction preceding the break-up, the tension and anxiety associated with the mortal illness, or the build-up towards the mother's final breakdown. A mother's absence does not, of itself, inevitably produce the gravest personal wounds. Providing always that the quality of the remaining relationships in which children grow up is one of sustained love and support, the young are apparently much less brittle, less vulnerable, than was previously supposed. Just as children, in general, seem to thrive as much in one-parent or 'blended' families as they do in conventional nuclear ones, so those whose mothers have been replaced by other loving care-takers are not inevitably set for a disastrous future life course.

Within the totality of their life careers, probably the greatest loss that most people ever experience is the death of their life partner. So massive is this kind of bereavement that, to begin with, people cannot even believe it. There is a sense of numb-ness, of shock; the widow, even if she has accepted it, is too dazed to take in the fact that her husband has really died. There is a sense that at any moment he may walk in through the door. At this early stage, people may also experience a kind of restless energy; there is, in fact, usually such a lot to do, so many arrangements to make, that little space is left for grief. It is only later, when the funeral is over, that the widow may find herself suddenly overwhelmed by anguish – an anguish which veers unpredictably between anger, self-reproach and an aching, yearning sense of loss. Ultimately, these painful feelings are inescapable. But people sometimes try desperately to forestall them. By quickly remarrying, by plunging oneself into engross-ing new activities – perhaps by these means one may fend off grief? Or, if you keep his room exactly as it was, maintain in every detail the routine you shared with him – if you do this, can you perhaps succeed in keeping him with you for ever? It seems that, in the end, strategies like these have no power to avert the impact of major personal loss, that they even rebound disastrously upon those who use them. Far from alleviating pain, such defensive manoeuvres only prolong it; five years after her husband's death, the widow who never really mourned him remains unhappy, dissatisfied, afflicted with a profound sense of emptiness and futility.

Major losses take a great deal of time before they can be accommodated. Widowed people themselves give ample testimony of this. Discussing the interviews they held with widows and widowers living in Boston, U.S.A., Colin Murray Parkes and Robert Weiss suggest why this must be so:

> Such changes always require the individual to discover discrepancies between the world that is now being faced and the world that, up to now, has been taken for granted. The amputee has to learn not to step on a foot that is not there, the newly blind must learn that it is useless to look toward the source of a noise, and, in like manner, the bereaved must stop including the dead in their plans, thoughts, and conversations. This process of learning is inevitably painful and time consuming. Time and again the amputee gets out of bed in the morning only to find himself sprawling on the floor, the blind person repeatedly peers through sightless eyes, and the widow or widower again and again forgets that the dead partner is gone for ever.*

In comforting the bereaved, people often assure them that time will heal the wound. Yet, though time is needed before major loss can be accommodated, time of itself does nothing towards such accommodation. Psychiatrists who have tried to help bereaved people sometimes use the term 'grief work'. Strange though this term may seem, it appears that it is only through *working* on our loss that we can ever really encompass it. What sort of work can this be?

To begin to answer this question, perhaps we should reflect on how those who have suffered major losses usually react. Most obviously, people who mourn tend to cry. And tears do seem to

---

* Parkes, C.M., and Weiss, R.S., *Recovery from Bereavement*, Basic Books, 1983.

help those in mourning, may even sometimes be a personal necessity: 'she must weep, or she will die'. If weeping is important in bereavement, this is perhaps because it involves open acknowledgment of grievous loss – it represents the declaration that, as a person, one has been gravely wounded, that the meaning of one's personal life course has been put in jeopardy.

Newly bereaved people often want to talk about the person they have lost, repeating the same story over and over again. Well meaning friends, listening yet again to the incident they have so often heard before, seeing their friend, who had seemed to be pulling out of it, break down again at the recollection – these friends may eventually try to forestall the endless rehearsal, which apparently does nothing but upset the bereaved person. Yet this rehearsing of painful memories is a crucial aspect of grief work. Only by confronting the poignancy of our losses is it possible to begin to accommodate them. Only if we dare to enter fully into what has been so dear, so intimate, so precious, and by entering into it, feel with anguish what we have lost – only if we do this, can we take the loss within ourselves, make it our own, incorporate it into the life we must continue to live. For this reason, what Parkes and Weiss call 'the fine-grained, almost filigree work with memory', is a vital part of encompassing personal loss.

The crucial importance, for further living, of painfully remembering, painfully reflecting upon the past is also suggested by the experience of a quite different group of people. Where personal relationships end, not through death, but through internal conflicts or pressures, those involved have, like the bereaved, necessarily sustained a major loss. One example of this situation is those whose marriages have broken down. While the widowed may find other people who are willing, at least up to a point, to listen, to support them in their grief work, this is likely to be much more difficult for the divorced. Through loyalty to the other partner, fearing to be drawn into the conflict or, perhaps, anxious about reverberations within their own marriages, most people are deeply unwilling to become involved in the angry, bitter or guilty grief of divorcees. Though it may not be impossible to work alone through recollections of a personally vital relationship – with all that one now feels about it – it is certainly very difficult. This means that, for many divorced people, no avenue is open for engaging adequately in grief work; they can only remain embittered, disillusioned, dwelling permanently in the failure of their hopes. And it is this unfinished business – the grief work not yet undertaken – which is apt to sabotage the new relationships which such people enter. Only where new partners – perhaps having themselves taken such work further – are able to support the painful process of going over and over the previous marriage, over and over how it came to fail, can the loss be finally encompassed and the person be able to make an investment in the present relationship. Only then, can the personal life-journey be resumed.

Accommodating loss does, in fact, mean more than recollecting the years spent intimately with another person, the particular vivid moments, the memorable conversations. Truly to work upon what has gone entails the long and difficult process of making personal sense of what it has all meant. A crude way of putting this is to say that a balance sheet has to be drawn up. What must urgently be balanced, for most people, is probably the way the loss came about. *Why* did he die, *why* did she leave me for another man? Many newly bereaved people spend a great deal of time – perhaps to the incomprehension, or the dismay, of others – repeatedly tracing the course of the last illness, the hours before the accident, the warning signs long previously. And it is just the same for those whose marriages have foundered. Over and over again they rehearse the events which preceded the final break-up: what happened, what was said. Perhaps an inevitable aspect of such thoughts are the agonizing 'if onlys'. If I had only realized . . .! If we hadn't quarrelled that very morning . . .! If only I had been more patient . . .! Though it may sometimes seem so, all this is not the tongue perversely probing the pain of an abscessed tooth. In talking with the widowed, Parkes and Weiss came to the conclusion that bereaved people cannot accept their loss until they have been able to create some 'account' of it – even if this is no more than the formulation that 'many people do die of this illness'.

The scope of the balance sheet, though, goes beyond the particular ways in which the vital relationship has ended. Somehow, the relationship itself has to be added up; one must know, finally, what it amounts to, in one's own life story. This, too, is a prolonged and a painful process. Relationships are, literally, ways of *being in relation*. When we lose them, we lose that relation to another; and that is why, in losing parents, husbands, intimate friends, children or lovers, we really do lose part of our selves. Yet to have encompassed within ourselves an *account* of the relationship – an account which has been deeply, honestly thought through, an account in which we acknowledge to ourselves all the minuses, as well as all the pluses – to have done this is, in some sense, not to have entirely lost what has ended.

Because we live in relation to others, an intimate relationship with another person entails a close access to that person's unique life, their particular personhood. Though we habitually think of people as isolated individuals, it may be truer to view ourselves as necessarily lodged with one another. Just as girls know the other half of the gender script and, in role play, can take that part with expertise – so the husband has the most detailed, the most intimate understanding of his wife's feelings, her way of reacting, how she sees things. He knows exactly what she will say to this, can foresee, with total accuracy, why she will not like that. Though it is she who speaks the lines, he could – were it not unnecessary and absurd – often say them for her. If she dies, not only has he lost the script in which his own part was guaranteed and given daily meaning. He has also lost the independent existence of the person whom, in all kinds of rich, intuitive, unexamined ways, he has lodged within himself. This, in some strange sense, means that he is now responsible for her – he carries her life within his own.

A fundamental part, therefore, of the account which must be worked out when we lose a vital relationship entails arriving at a summation of the meaning of that person's life, seen in the round. This can take a very long time. Here is Colette reflecting on her father, many years after his death:

As we approached the village, my father would resume his
defensive humming, and no doubt we looked very happy,
since to look happy was the highest compliment we paid
each other. But was not everything about us, the gathering dusk, the wisps of smoke trailing across the sky, and
the first flickering star, as grave and restless as ourselves?
And in our midst a man, banished from the elements that
had once sustained him, brooded bitterly.

Yes, bitterly; I am sure of that now. It takes time for
the absent to assume their true shape in our thoughts.
After death they take on a firmer outline and then cease to
change. 'So that's the real you? Now I see, I never understood you.' It is never too late, since now I have fathomed
what formerly my youth hid from me: my brilliant, cheer-
ful father harboured the profound sadness of those who
have lost a limb.*

To love is to suffer. Yet, it is better to have loved and
lost . . . Paradoxically, it does seem to be those people whose
relationships have been deepest, richest, most intimate, who
are best able, ultimately, to encompass their loss within them,
rather than being permanently crippled by it. For those whose
relational position was more complicated, more ambivalent, or
more limited, true mourning is evidently much more difficult.
And, similarly, it is the lives which seem to have been best lived,
most fulfilled, most individually shaped, whose ending we can
more easily bear than those which seem to have remained
cramped, unfulfilled, undeveloped. This is also, perhaps, what is
felt by those who are facing their own death. The bitterest regrets
which dying people express are those that arise from a sense of
waste – of opportunities not taken, of risks not dared, a life of
getting and spending, of safety rather than commitment, a life
which, in retrospect, looks petty or cowardly. In the adding-up of
how one has lived, the urgent question must always be, what has
my life amounted to – has it, in the end, counted?

* Colette, *Earthly Paradise*, Secker & Warburg, 1966.

In terminal illness, many people do engage in this kind of personal stock-taking. But, unless we experience some kind of crisis in our lives, probably few of us otherwise do so. In particular, we do not generally accord this kind of thoughtful, painful attention to the phases of life we are leaving behind. As we leave school at last, and eagerly, impatiently enter the world of work, of money, of adult freedoms and independence, we seldom spend much time looking back over what we are leaving behind. We are much too busy planning, looking ahead. But it may be that it is just this contemptuous disregard for our past experience – the life we had, the self we were – which renders it entirely and irrevocably lost to us. Because we never realize what it is we are leaving, we never encompass it within ourselves. Later, we find that something precious, belonging to that time, has gone from us for ever. We cannot recapture our vividness of feeling: like Hopkins's future Margaret, we have lost our earlier sensibilities. Somehow the way we came to constitute our new, older selves disallowed the acknowledgment of the past as still part of the present. As a result, though we feel there is something vital missing – something we once had – we seem to find no personal access to it. Yet conversely, if, as we experience our changing lives, we relive, we reflect, we mull over what we are leaving behind, then, in some sense, we continue to possess it.

Logically, the certain knowledge that we shall die ought to facilitate constant personal stock-taking, for we should all be living our lives within the conscious perspective of their finite limits. But logically is not psychologically. Nearly everybody who tries to think about their own death finds it difficult to take in, to assimilate its reality. It seems impossible to absorb the fact that one day we shall simply end. Yet, as many people have noted, in societies other than our own an awareness of death is not merely part of everyday human reality; the fact of death is also integrated within an essentially positive, affirmative framework of meaning.

Some years ago I organized a workshop on the topic of death. I wanted to explore, with others, the reality of our own future deaths and what kinds of personal implications this held. In workshops on other topics that I had run, both men and women had attended; but in this case, only women came. This seemed to suggest that women might be readier than men to try to face their own death. There is an American psychologist, David Bakan, who sees human life as a duality between two contrasting directions – agency on the one hand, and communion on the other.* Agency refers to volition, to all the aspects of life that have to do with intention, control, purposeful action. Communion, on the other hand, involves sharing between people, living in relation to others, being one with another. In this society, as Bakan argues, it is men whose lives are generally expected to be governed by agency; women's being is typically seen much more in terms of communion. If we think of death in relation to these two modes, it is, perhaps, much easier to reconcile with communion than with agency. Most people view death as something which happens to us – something over which we have no control. As such, it represents a final and unanswerable challenge to the idea that we are in charge of things. We can, however, make more sense of death in terms of communion. Many of the ways in which people see possibilities of transcending their own death are essentially those of communion. Living on in the lives of one's children, identification with the future of humanity, oneness with God or nature – all these involve escaping the limits of personal individuality, by sharing the lives, the concerns, the spirit of other beings. If it is the case that men in general find the prospect of their own death even more unthinkable than do women, this may be because a life in which agency is the supreme, governing principle, to the exclusion of communion, has no place in which death can be encompassed.

Yet for all of us, it is surely very difficult to assimilate the reality of our own future deaths, at least more than momentarily. Ironically, it may be that the real grimness, even the horror of many ways of dying are themselves the by-product of our reluctance to face death. The work of hospices for the terminally ill show us that dying *need* not be as we usually make it. Evidently

* Bakan, D., *The Duality of Human Existence*, Rand McNally, 1966.

the sense of lonely anguish, of grotesque pretences, of fears unshared, of loss of dignity, of personal diminution – all these proceed from a view of the dying as representing the ultimate threat to the living. It is this view which governs our usual provision for those with terminal illness, a provision which strips them of their personal identity, places them in the sterile world of the hospital, limits their contact with others' lives and disengages them from personal relationships. Because to die is to 'fail' medical treatment, dying people must be hidden behind screens. This is one side of the same coin which also seeks at all costs to hide the truth from the dying person, and so violates the respect, the responsibility to which as human beings we are all entitled.

One effect of this treatment of those who are dying must be to remove the possibility of the kind of grief work which – just like the bereaved – those in this situation surely need to do. If we think of the kinds of actions which, in human societies, have often been expected and encouraged in people facing death, they seem to entail ways of working out a personal balance sheet, defining a personal account of one's own life. People need to put their affairs in order, to make a confession, to set right an old wrong, to say what should be said but has never yet been said, to make gifts to relatives, friends or causes. All these are, perhaps, ways in which – as far as it can be done – a life is made complete, given a final kind of account. And this embraces how one's own life shall be defined, in the farewells that others make to it. The choices that people make as to their own funeral arrangements – the music to be played, the prayers to be said, the letter to be read out, the place of burial or the disposal of ashes – all these are kinds of statements about the deepest levels of meaning in the life one has led. Most fundamentally, they represent an affirmation. And perhaps it is the inability to affirm the meaning of one's own life which is ultimately most terrible. There can be no more final expression of despair than that of Michael Henchard, in Hardy's *Mayor of Casterbridge*, who, in his last letter, asks, 'And let no man remember me.'

12 THREE METAPHORS OF LIVING

In the account which has made up this book so far, some of our usual ways of understanding human life over time have been questioned. Although we typically think of the life-span as consisting of three different qualitatively distinct phases, people, it has been suggested, are recognizably the same regardless of what age they are. Nor is the meaning of time across life necessarily something linear, involving progression to a peak, followed by decline. To view what we ordinarily call deviance from a different perspective is one way in which to see the limits, and the arbitrariness, of our usual portrayal of proper kinds of life course. And if we examine some of the spheres of our experience – as embodied men and women, growing up in family groupings or experiencing losses in our lives – it becomes evident that the people we become, the life courses we run, are not the product of simple mechanical determinants, but come about through the vital yet delicate process of giving meaning to our own and each other's lives.

At its most profound, the meaning of human life is carried in metaphor. For few of us are the metaphors we live by explicit; we do not usually have any conscious awareness of living out anything beyond what seems to be our literal experience. Yet ultimately, it is the metaphorical sense we make of our living that gives the journey its direction, its sense of progression or development, its turning points, changes and passages, the meaning of its beginning and its end.

There is surely no limit to the number of metaphors which are possible. Different ways of seeing the human life-span imply their own distinctive metaphorical models. Even official psychology – however scientific we may believe it to be – is in the end rooted in a particular vision. That vision can never be proved true – or untrue, for that matter. What counts is not its 'truth', but whether, as a metaphor of life, it enlarges or diminishes our living.

Despite the variety of metaphors available, any particular society must impose its own constraints on what seems possible, believable. In our own present-day culture there are, perhaps, three kinds of vision which potentially encapsulate, for most of us, our sense of our lives, our human progress. It is these three metaphors which, in this last chapter, we shall be exploring.

THE GAME OF CARDS

If there is one metaphor which fits most easily into our society, which is most readily encompassed by our social structures and institutional framework, it is perhaps the metaphor that human life represents a game of cards. Within this image, to be born any particular human being is to be dealt some of the most important cards of the hand that, in living, one must play. To be born into a 'good' family, a family which is middle class rather than working class, white rather than black, settled, respectable, prosperous rather than impoverished and insecure – this is to start life with certain key cards. Gender and physique represent other kinds of suit, in which the male card is preferable, but in which card combinations are also important – different kinds of embodiment being cards which enhance or diminish the value of the gender card. Other cards in the hand are not available at birth, but are acquired later, particularly during childhood and adolescence. They represent factors which will affect later life chances, such as exam passes, kind of schooling, early pregnancy or involvement with the police.

In this metaphor, it is only grown-ups who can really play the game. Not until childhood and adolescence have passed is it clear what cards are in one's hand. To the inheritance of good and bad cards provided through the lottery of birth, one has added others, acquired partly through circumstances, partly through one's own conduct. A final, crucial card in the hand is that of individual character – a joint product, as it is usually seen in this context, of heredity and early circumstances. Again, what value this card has – what it represents in assets and liabilities – will not be fully clear until adulthood is reached. And just as young people are as yet unready to take their part in the real game of life, so too the old are disqualified from playing by their age. In being old, not only have they lost certain key cards necessary to the players – cards defining adult power, adult status. They have also lost access to many of the vital arenas in which the game must be played.

The game itself is, of course, a game of competition. Certain players will win – perhaps spectacularly – while others will lose. That is the essential character of the game: no player can win unless other players lose. Some players, whose initial endowment was fortunate, whom chance has blessed with favourable circumstances, or many gifts, start the game with an excellent hand. Others have been dealt a much less advantageous one, or perhaps have already thrown away the good cards they started with by rash behaviour in youth. But, despite the inequalities of the hands held, there is no knowing who is actually going to win the game of life. A good hand does not inevitably bring success, nor a bad one, failure. Winning the game depends on *playing your cards right*.

What is entailed in playing your cards right? Most basically, playing well depends on knowing the value of the cards you hold. It is not enough to have good cards if you do not realize that they are aces, or in what circumstances they can be played to best advantage. You will only squander your trumps, and waste the valuable opportunities open to you. But it is equally essential to understand your low-value cards. Unless you have taken your liabilities into account, they will betray you; by playing them at the wrong time, you will fatally expose your weak position. In all this, tactics and strategies are crucial. To play your cards right means developing a plan of campaign which will maximize the assets you hold and safeguard your vulnerabilities as far as is possible. So in adulthood, the good player plans ahead, evolving a life strategy which will realistically match goals with personal capacities, take advantage of every possible opportunity, and avoid situations which might expose personal weaknesses.

But other life strategies, other tactics are also possible. Like poker, the game of life allows its players to bluff. If you have the nerve and the skill for it, you can pass off your basically poor hand as though you held all the trumps, and other people will never discover how weak your position really is. By the confident attitude you assume, you can successfully hide your disreputable background, your lack of material resources, your succession of failed marriages, your low occupational status. You can present an altogether different social image, and people will take you for what you seem to be. By this strategy, you may actually end up a winner. And different kinds of players do, in this metaphor, adopt different sorts of tactics in the game they play. For women and for men, the game is to be differently played. While men are expected to adopt relatively straightforward tactics – to play their cards openly and directly – women are expected to adopt more devious manoeuvres. Though for both genders the game is one of competition, of gaining power and advantage over others, women, as women, should not *seem* to be playing it. Instead, their tactics should be covert. By adopting a helpless, passive stance, by coaxing, or provoking others into taking action, they gain their tricks without apparently trying to – without making any effort on their own behalf.

Nor need strategies only be on an individual basis. In the game of cards, the game of life, people may act as partners. The partnership may be a regular one, lasting throughout the whole play, or it may be more limited, with partners changing after each round. But whether long-term or temporary, the two players use their hands to combine forces for the game. In their alliance, each will use his cards to compensate or cover for his partner's weaknesses and liabilities. And each will try to match her own play to that of her partner's – to adopt strategies and tactics which are mutually consonant. The better, therefore, that each already knows or can accurately sum up the other's assets, liabilities and way of playing, the more effective will be their double game.

The game is one from which children and old people are debarred. It is the exclusive preserve of adults. But not of every adult. For some, there is early disqualification; the mentally handicapped are clearly unable to master the rules of the game, and cannot compete at all. Other people, 'criminals', break the rules – or, perhaps more critically, get caught breaking them. They are seen to have marked the cards, to have hidden an ace up their sleeve. For this, they too are excluded. Another group of potential players themselves declare their own reluctance, and choose to opt out of the game. Others take part, but seem not to grasp the rules; their game apparently follows different principles altogether. Those who play with them become increasingly puzzled and distressed; finally, such individuals are judged, as disturbed people, to be unfit for further play.

If there is scope, in the life-game of cards, for a variety of tactics and strategies, some choice also exists, for most people, in the kind of game to be played. Among the several social worlds which we inhabit, one may be declared the crucial arena of play, while others are defined as outside the game. Some people choose to play in public spheres of action, others, in private ones. For certain men in our society, for instance, family life represents a non-game world, a relief from competitive play. The real game is being played out at work, where institutional structures already exist to mark out progress, and success or failure are conspicuous. But for other men, the cards that count are those one can play at home; the game is, perhaps, a deadly one, in which the stakes are marital domination, marital subservience, the respect or contempt of the children. In this arena, the rules of the game are not publicly available, but must be worked out within each particular family grouping. Rules may be initially derived from those which operated when the adults were children, in their own family contexts. But, for the game to be played properly, the rules must be agreed by all those involved, as players or spectators. It is when, sometimes, younger members of the family begin to question the rules, that things may disintegrate and the game becomes unplayable.

For many people, the metaphor of life as a game of cards would, perhaps, fit quite well with personal experience. Our society is, to a large extent, set up in ways which endorse such a

view. Hierarchies of power, status, competence extend throughout life; from an early age, children are aware of their own
position on the social scale. Just as, in schooling, pupils are
defined as doing well only because others are defined as doing
badly, so, later, men and women, in order to be successful, must
compete with each other for property, accomplishments, social
rank and prestige. By the time they enter the phase we mark off
as old age, people are, as a rule, very keenly aware of how they
have done, as individuals, in the social competition – of whether
it is as winners or as losers that they have ended up.

Given that, in so many ways, life in our society seems to be a
matter of constant desperate mutual competition, the metaphor
of a card game is perhaps not an inaccurate one. It may be true
that, in order to survive, we all have, to some extent, to live our
lives in these terms. This metaphor also captures an aspect of
human life which resonates particularly for the socially disadvantaged – the inequality of the hands dealt. Although those whose
situation in life is secure, comfortable, privileged, are seldom
much concerned about this aspect, it is a highly salient one for
people whose initial handicaps seem to disqualify them from the
game, even before they start to play.

Granted that this metaphor expresses many of the dimensions
which govern our particular society, nevertheless it is one that
probably appeals much more to some people than to others. It has
been remarked earlier that the principle of agency – of purpose
and self-direction – plays a larger part in the lives of most men
than it does generally in those of women. On the whole, it is men
whom we expect to take control of the courses of their lives, to
plan effectively for the future, to be responsible for events. And,
on the whole, men do incorporate this expectation within their
personal stance to life. Whereas, for instance, most young
women, at eighteen, feel unable to forecast their future lives
beyond about a five-year span, eighteen-year-old men, by contrast, can typically predict the lives they hope to be leading
twenty years hence.

To build one's life upon one's own personal agency may be, in
our society, to gain the admiration of others, and to respect

oneself, as a proper kind of man. Yet it is a costly way to live. There is now ample documentation of the physical consequences of such a stance – the early coronaries, the chronic tension, which go with the constant striving after ever-greater achievements, ever-enhanced success. Since chance events and the behaviour of others are an ever-present unavoidable threat to the single-minded pursuit of one's own destiny, the attempt at total personal control can only represent a hostile stance towards life, and is, in the end, inevitably doomed.

The metaphor of a card-game essentially endorses the standard psychological assumptions we generally make about human life. It portrays people as fundamentally individualistic. Even if individuals make temporary alliances with each other, this is only for the purpose of acting *against* others more effectively. The metaphor incorporates the view of life as basically competitive. Different human lives must be measured against the same parameters. In these terms, many will be found wanting. There is no room for those who cannot or will not abide by the rules: such people can only be dismissed as deviant human beings.

Little scope for dignity seems to exist in this metaphor of life. Most people will end up losers. Even those declared winners may find their success hollow or precarious. The only way, perhaps, of living out this metaphor without grossly diminishing one's humanity, is to develop a personal style of play. Or, perhaps, the heart, the zest, the conviction we put into our lives can make them count, regardless of the outcome of our efforts; it matters not who won or lost, but how you played the game. Or, finally, it may be that human dignity resides in the ironic stance which, as losers, we can take towards our loss. We failed; yet we ourselves can mock that failure. That way, we can, perhaps, respect ourselves.

This metaphor does, of course, have its own perspective on time – and it is a dismal one. Within its terms, the three phases of human life remain differentiated. As in our standard psychology, it is only adulthood which really counts. Children stand by, envious spectators of the game they cannot yet enter, picking up what they can of the tricks, the manoeuvres in which the players engage. As for the old, the numerous losers are left with their shame; all they can do is warn their children of the strategies that do not pay off. Even winners have only the memory of their past successes to warm them, and their strategies, their successes are soon forgotten by others, surpassed by the next generation of players. The reach of time across human life has little richness, little significance, to offer. Relations between the generations, as between contemporaries, are those of envy, rivalry. The lives of others, lived long ago, serve as no more than early versions of the same game – despised, perhaps, for the limited arenas, the primitive tactics by which they were played out.

THE NATURAL CYCLE

In the first section of this chapter, we considered the metaphor of human life as a game of cards. Basically, it seemed to represent a diminishing rather than enhancing view. Suppose we envisaged our lives in metaphorical terms which were as unlike the card-player as we could imagine? We might then, perhaps, see ourselves as living out a natural cycle.

If we looked at human life in this way, the features which make up our experience, the meaning of particular life periods, the significance of changes and transitions, our whole sense of our life courses – all these things would appear very differently. You are, let us imagine, a plant, a shrub, a tree. There you stand, rooted in the soil within which, also, grow other kinds of plant. That soil nourishes you; but so also do the sunlight and the rain that fall upon you. You have your seasons, each of which is different, all of which are necessary. In spring, you emerge into visible life, you put forth young shoots which are green and tender. As the days lengthen into summer, you grow stronger. Your limbs become rounded out, and more diversified. The little buds swell, opening into flowers. Then comes autumn. Your decorative petals have all fluttered away, leaving only the seeds, the fruit; these seeds ripen quietly, steadily, until they drop to the ground below. During this season, your covering of leaves begins to change. As the leaves die, they turn from green to brown, yellow, or russet. For a little while they hang there, then they too fall to the ground. In winter you stand for a time, quite bare; your outlines, your essential structure, are clearer than they have ever been before. As the nights lengthen, and the frost encases you, your twigs become brittle and drop off. Gradually, too, the main stems of your body develop cracks and start to fall apart. By the end of winter you stand there no longer. There is only a little mound of leafmould, a few scattered pieces of wood, to show where once you stood. But with the coming of spring, around that spot new shoots appear, uncurling their heads from the seeds which once dropped from your boughs.

Unlike the card-game metaphor, that of the natural cycle emphasizes transience, and enriches the meaning of changes over time. If human life is a game of cards, its basic significance is single, and static. Early and late life play no real part in that significance; their role is merely that of exclusion from the game. But if life is a natural cycle, then it entails phases of living which are both interdependent, and qualitatively distinctive. Spring could not happen if autumn had not gone before; there would be no new forms of human life if older generations had not come to maturity, and created possibilities. The glory of summer is dependent on the existence of winter. Only if early life has been allowed gradually to grow, in secret, under its covering of snow, of frost-hardened earth, can the adult plant come to its full maturity, reveal the splendours of its natural form.

Within this metaphor, every phase of life has its own meaning, its own dignity. There is grace and delicacy, as well as promise, in youthful forms of life, and loveliness in the flowering of youth into manhood, womanhood. But not only are human spring and summer to be gloried in, as development towards a kind of peak. Middle age is also rich in meaning, as the period in which each life bears its essential fruit, offers its own contribution. At this life period, the image, though different from that of younger phases, may have its own kind of magnificence. The middle-aged person, like the maple with its scarlet leaves, can possess a character which is altogether striking. And the winter of life – treated so dismissively in the card-playing metaphor – here takes on its special, distinctive value. Like the bare outlines of a beech tree, the nobility of a person's character is not fully apparent until old age, when all the inessentials of life have been stripped away.

In the card-playing metaphor, our human embodiments have little significance. Our bodies are merely one of the cards we have to play: a trump, if we happen to be the right shape for the woman we are, a low card, if our physique fails to meet the conventional gender stereotype. By contrast, if we see our lives as a natural cycle, it is through our embodiments that we express their deepest meaning. The changes in our physical selves, as we go through life, mirror the essential character of each life phase. It is in childhood, when our bodies are at their most pliant, that our personal selves are most open to moulding: as the twig is bent, so we will take our unique psychological character from the experience of our early years. And as, in childhood, our bones are slender, easily broken, our bodies dependent, for their proper growth, on adequate nourishment – so we cannot hope to achieve psychological wholeness, but will remain permanently stunted, if, as children, we suffered major disasters, or grew up insufficiently loved and cared for.

This view of human embodiment does, in fact, demand respect for our bodies, and for the bodily changes to which we are subject. Physical transitions and the time at which they occur are accepted as natural, and therefore right. And the psychological meaning which such changes carry is profound, sacrosanct. As the woman's body becomes reproductively mature, so there is a time to love, and to bear children from that love. When her body reaches the menopause, it is time to refrain from loving. To ignore these transitions is to ride roughshod over what is fundamentally, deeply, appropriate. Denying the reproductive meaning of sexuality, by the use of artificial contraceptives, continuing an active sexual life beyond the menopause or using hormones to mitigate its effects – this is interfering with what is natural, defying the proper courses of our lives.

Because this metaphor stresses the continuity of human life forms with the rest of the natural order, its most central meanings derive from the physical aspects of existence which we share with plants, trees, other animals. This gives it a crucial emphasis on physical reproduction. The natural cycle is, ultimately, a cycle through which the species is reproduced. Our lives unfold, as the particular nature, carried in our heredity, comes to maturity. Alone in a field of buttercups, a foxglove seed still cannot grow to be anything but a foxglove. With our families, and especially with our parents, we have the closest possible affinities. To see things in these terms means that producing and bringing up children assumes the very greatest significance, represents the highest purpose in our lives. From this perspective, the family is, perhaps, by far the most significant social institution, and parents, society's most profoundly important members.

It is, in fact, from this perspective that the metaphor of life as natural cycle takes its definition of certain kinds of people, and certain sorts of human life courses, as deviant. Within the card-game metaphor, normality is narrowly defined. There is only one set of rules, and these must be strictly followed; no deviations of any kind can be allowed. This means that many people, in different ways, qualify for deviance. By contrast, the natural-cycle metaphor has a far more generous view of human experience and human diversity. One aspect of this is that the life-force is essentially robust and tenacious. By and large, the natural order does withstand the vicissitudes, the adverse circumstances of life. The little silver birch bends, but does not break in the raging wind; the grass, brown after months of drought, assumes its natural green after a single night of summer rain. Devastated at rejection by the woman he loved, Schubert yet went on to compose the most serene, the most shimmering music he had ever written. And, in the natural world, there is room for many species, and many variations within each species. A weed is only a flower in the wrong place. And it is the very diversity of form and colour – the endless variety of human beings – that gives life its beauty and vitality.

Yet if the natural order gives a place to many different sorts of people, it cannot easily or fully accommodate those individuals who violate its fundamental principles. People who remain childless, who abjure conventional family life, are seen to stand solitary, barren, like gaunt figures amidst the glory of a flowering orchard. Men who are 'unmasculine', women whose image, whose behaviour, do not express 'true femininity' – these are plants which have somehow grown wrong, become warped. And those whose sexuality is homosexual, not heterosexual, are more unnatural still, and can only be regarded as representing a perversion of life form.

In this metaphor, human life is not something which we construct for ourselves; it is our own nature unfolding. Just as we can realize what is the distinctive character of a violet as against a primrose, by observing the form the two flowers take, so we can know our own human nature only by seeing and experiencing how things are in our own society. It is through witnessing all the ways in which men, as people, are so different from women, that we come to understand the natural meaning of gender. As we see, in instance after instance, how working-class and black-skinned people live their lives in contexts which are different, and humbler, than those of white, middle-class people – so we learn that race and social class naturally involve living in differentiated ways. We find, too, that human existence naturally, inevitably, entails certain kinds of behaviour. We have only to look around us, only to reflect on the course of human history, to realize that people are naturally aggressive, naturally given to greed, competition and rapaciousness – as well as to heroism, dedication, self-sacrifice. Just as it is useless to bewail the fact that nature is red in tooth and claw, so we cannot, realistically, hope to eradicate human violence and exploitation.

If we view human life as a natural cycle rather than as a game of cards, then change, loss, transience become aspects of experience which we can accommodate – and accommodate as, in some sense, enriching rather than destructive. We can, too, escape the pitfalls of a metaphor which emphasizes agency to the exclusion of communion. To be a card-player is to live in a state of perpetual tension and anxiety. We cannot really dwell in the present; we live only in the future. Because we ourselves are responsible for our lives, we must constantly plan ahead, take stock of our position, monitor the manoeuvres of opposing players, develop strategies in secret. Other people are at best temporary allies, more characteristically, enemies and rivals. But if our lives are part of the natural order, then we all stand together. As human beings, we pass through the same elemental transitions – and they are the same transitions as were experienced by all those who lived before us, and will come after us. We know, in our fundamentally similar nature, the same vicissitudes of experience; it is to the same joys, the same tragedies, that we are all subject. Our human nature does not divide, but unites us. And fundamentally, the human lives that we experience are not the product of our own deliberate plans, our own conscious purposes and efforts. They come about through the simple unfolding of the common humanity we all share. As individuals, we are essentially part of a larger order, an order in which, through our own lives, we contribute something to the general richness. Our lives make up the ground in which others can live, and each of us has our part to play in how life continually renews itself. Yet, despite the larger vision which this metaphor carries, its emphasis on human nature inevitably entails an endorsement of the social status quo. If what is possible in human life is only to be taken from the way things are, then all the existing inequalities, injustices, cruelties and oppression of our current society can only be perpetuated. Not until we can envisage new possibilities, evolve new visions of human life, can we transcend the limits of our present ways of living.

LIFE AS STORY

Bored with the long wait in the supermarket queue, a young mother studies the elderly woman in front of her. She notes hair, clothes, bag, wedding ring, the items in the basket. She watches the woman as she reaches the checkout, observes how she packs away her groceries, handles her money, speaks to the cashier. A widow, she concludes. Probably been on her own for some years. Manages on her pension, but has seen better days. Lives alone, with just her cat for company. So the young woman sums up the other. And it is all true. Yet this portrait says absolutely nothing about the particular, the unique life at issue. What can the by-stander possibly know of the trials, the tragedies, the splendours, of such a life? How could she guess that the many years of married life were darkened by the husband's increasing physical violence? That this violence, rarely glimpsed by the children, totally unsuspected by others, has surrounded the greater part of this woman's adult life with a wall of shame and secrecy? Or that now, with the ticket to Australia received from her son last week, this elderly woman stands on the brink of a new phase in her life? That she looks forward, with strange and poignant feelings, to meeting her grandchildren, one of whom, in photographs, looks so exactly like her husband looked in youth?

Each of us lives a story that is ours alone. It is this story which gives our lives their essential shape, defines their heights, their plateaux, their declines, marks out their movement, direction, changes in direction. In living, we tell our own stories. Nor are these stories merely a catalogue of the events which occur within our life-span. As the authors of our personal story, it is we who must select, from the myriad happenings we witness daily, what belongs to the story and what lies outside. Only we can weave what we select into the narrative, only we ourselves can link what is happening now with what has passed, and what may yet happen in our lives. As authors, we have agency. In this metaphor, human beings have powers of creation and responsibility which they do not possess as part of a natural cycle. Yet this is an agency which is not quite like that of the card-player. Certainly, as human beings, we act in our lives. We engage ourselves in events, with our own intentions, our own purposes. We initiate things. We launch and pursue our projects. Yet in the end, we do not control outcomes; we are not, finally, in charge of how things will turn out. As story-tellers, we are not free to construct whatever plot we choose.

Your central, most sustained, most personally resonant theme is intimately linked with the life of another person, who is suddenly snatched from you by illness, accident, betrayal. Or the life quest you are pursuing in your own context is brought drastically, irrevocably to an end by political exile. From all the richness of meaning in your own cultural setting, from the position of prominence and respect which you have gained – you are violently thrust into an alien country, into strange territory where you are nobody, or, if you are noticed at all, it is as an object of others' hatred and contempt.

The vicissitudes of life to which, as human beings, we are all subject, pose great challenges to the stories we live out. Can we incorporate into our personal stories what is unlooked for, regretted, horrifying? Can we use such events as raw material from which the story will develop, out of which our lives will, in the end, gain greater depth? Or must the author's voice falter and fall silent – or else, speak again of a story which is totally new, altogether out of keeping, incorporating nothing of what was heard before?

If we do not exactly write the plots of our lives, nevertheless it is we alone who create our own stories. Agency lies not in governing what shall happen to us, but in creating what we make of what happens. We ourselves construct the meaning of our story. And because it is we who live out that story, the kind of meaning we give it has the most intimate, and the most serious, consequences for how we live. In our perspective on our own past history, in our anticipation of the future, in making our way through the infinite complexity of encounters and events – we have only our personal story to guide us. Though it is we who shape our stories, those stories also shape us – our selves and our lives.

Being the author of your own life story – this is how many people would see things. Even for adults, viewing life from a relatively powerful vantage-point, it is common to feel oneself the victim of circumstances, the recipient of the blows, or the gifts, of fate or chance. Things turn out one way or the other; there is nothing much to be done about it. You happen to be lucky or unlucky in life. It is, in a sense, life which lives you, rather than the other way round. This is, of course, one kind of story. And though it is a story which denies the essentially creative character of human life, nevertheless it can offer, sometimes, its own resigned, stoical dignity.

Most fundamentally, stories are differentiated by the vision they offer of human life. There are, it has been suggested (for instance, Barnes, citing Schafer),* four basic kinds of vision: comic, romantic, tragic and ironic. In our usual psychology about the human meaning of time, we do, perhaps, reserve the first two of these for earlier life phases. To see life according to the comic vision is to view it as basically safe and secure, to assume that all will, in the end, be well, that human affairs can be set right, that problems can be laughed at, because they do not pose a final threat to happiness. This is the life view which we offer children – in the stories of books, comics, television programmes. Yet it is a philosophy to which probably rather few adults in our present-day society would subscribe. And perhaps, in the sense they construct of human life, many children assimilate more from the stories of the adults around them, than from the material offered them as young, supposedly 'unrealistic' human beings.

If the happy ever after is seen as suiting childhood, it is the romantic vision to which adolescents are expected to subscribe. This views life in terms of an ardent idealism. Human affairs will be transformed by pure love, by selfless commitment, by personal integrity. Adult men and women, who generally look, perhaps, with mixed contempt and wistfulness upon such a view, would believe it to be untenable: compromises must be made, the golden age will never finally be achieved in human life. Yet teenagers who are similarly sceptical, who derive their vision from the 'real' social world, rather than from the quest for the Holy Grail, are felt to be prematurely, shockingly cynical. By the same token, men and women whose vision of life is essentially romantic, tend to be dismissed as naive, lacking in maturity. Yet lives lived within this vision, as within the comic vision, have a freshness and innocence, and their own kind of validity.

* Barnes, B., 'Doubts and certainties in practising psychotherapy', chapter in Pilgrim, D. (ed.), *Psychology and Psychotherapy: Current Trends and Issues*, Routledge & Kegan Paul, 1983.

Myths, legends, literature, history – in these public stories all four kinds of vision have served as sources of inspiration. Stories that are felt to be particularly moving, specially illuminating, have often been informed by the tragic or the ironic visions – the visions which many people would see as the most mature. Both visions emphasize the limits of human control, the inevitable sufferings of human life. The tragic view rests on the acceptance of pain and loss, the refusal to gloss over these aspects of living. The more detached ironic view offers a sense of the ultimate uncertainty of human life. For all that, in their different ways, these two views stress what is painful, problematic, for all that they abjure the comfort of simple solutions, both visions can, nevertheless, allow their own sense of personal affirmation.

If we look, in other terms, at human life stories, it seems that these are often the story of a journey. *Pilgrim's Progress* is a fable in which many people can find meaning. In our conventional psychology, too, the life course constitutes a sort of journey. Yet this journey is, perhaps, ultimately disappointing. The heights, invisible to children climbing laboriously up, to old people slithering down the other side, are mastered only in the adult years. To men and women, living out this story, these heights may turn out hardly worth the effort. Gazing about them, looking round at the flat, unexciting landscape, they can only ask, 'Is this all there is?' If this particular journey proves, in the end, so bleak to those who make it, perhaps it is because, in travelling it, we go in a straight line, always in the same direction. Journeys that have greater possibilities are more mysterious; they entail detours, blind alleys, maze-like meanderings, changes of direction, as well as unforeseen turnings, unexpected vistas. Travelling may be more important than arriving. But the destination, if it is attained, is perhaps the point at which the journey began. Like T.S. Eliot's traveller, we arrive at the place we started from, and know it for the first time. To live out this kind of story is to see our childhood, not as a place we have put behind us, but as a landscape which is still ours, to which we can return, in which, through the further living we have done, we shall find still richer meaning.

In the stories that, as individuals, we live out, we do, of course, draw constant inspiration from the stories of others. Our own lives are informed by the stories we read. A convincing, moving autobiography, or work of fiction, enlarges our own perspective – allows new possibilities for the stories we ourselves might tell. But the stories we encounter are also those of living persons. It is, perhaps, in the stories they offer, that parents have their essential impact. And throughout our lives, we encounter others whose personal stories inspire or depress us, excite our awe, our horror, our imagination, who change our conception of what our own life story might be.

Within this metaphor, there is a strong sense of communion; our life stories touch, constantly and intricately, those of others. Personal stories are seldom stories of solitary, isolated individuals. Your own life is felt to constitute one part of a collective life; in your own journey you take further the struggles, the movement, of a much larger human group. Your story reaches into the past, takes up themes in lives already lived. Something in your own story will, perhaps, be taken up in the future lives of others. In our personal relationships, too, we are not merely the spectators of the lives of others. Through our engagement with children, friends, intimates, we engage ourselves with their stories, we believe, follow, support, further, the story they are living out. Falling in love is, perhaps, the thrilling sense that our own story would be infinitely enriched by that kind of engagement. If you could only conjoin your two narratives, how wonderfully they might both develop! And when we lose an intimate relationship, not only do we lose a uniquely understanding, sympathetic audience, who has known, and helped us tell, such a large part of our own personal story. We also lose someone who was committed to taking the story forward, jointly writing the next chapters of our lives in terms which confirmed and elaborated what had gone before. Part of this loss is that such a person can now never know how the story went on.

Sometimes, though, people find no audience for their personal stories. So harrowing, or so shameful, does your story seem that you dare not entrust it to others. Your public story is, perhaps, quite different from the personal story that, privately, you tell yourself. Or, though you try to tell other people about the enduring themes in your life, it seems they cannot really understand; your story is, apparently, incomprehensible to others. The story made sense in the family where you grew up; but now, it seems, no one else can grasp it. Or the story you are living out is at odds with what is expected in your society. The price of social non-conformity may be the bewilderment of others. People defined socially as deviant, are, in this metaphor, those whose stories flout the usual conventions of fiction, are difficult to follow, or seem not to be stories at all. These situations are all personally costly. Just as most deeply bereaved people need the support of others in constructing an account of their loss – a major part of their own story – so, for few of us, is it possible to create a personal life story in total isolation. Yet, as those who enter psychotherapy can sometimes find, the committed audience of just one other person can, no matter at what stage, allow the construction of life meanings.

If parents, friends, intimates, psychotherapists can support and further our personal life stories, then enemies can threaten and undermine them. By holding up to ridicule our deepest themes, by sabotaging the story's working out, by proving that our life is better told by a quite different story – by these acts of hatred and betrayal they can produce a personal destruction from which, as authors, we sometimes never recover. Brainwashing, the deliberate breaking down of people, rests on the systematic destruction of their personal stories. For victims of this kind of psychological assault, every facet of the story by which they live is subjected to attack; their most basic interpretations – the foundations of the story – are shown to be untenable. They find that the narrative in which they confidently linked past with present, within which they planned future actions, made sense of what they experienced – this narrative has disintegrated, leaving only a terrifying chaos. In such a situation, people reach eagerly for the alternative story offered them, the chance to find coherence and meaning in a world where nothing makes sense any more.

Though most men and women yield to brainwashing, there

are a few who have proved able to resist it. They are, at first sight, a strange collection of people: Turkish infantrymen, British army officers, Jehovah's Witnesses. But there is something which all these people have in common. All have experienced a prolonged and thorough acquisition of a very distinctive group identity – a life-long identity which marks out its members as indelibly different and elite, as carrying always with them the confirmation, the approval, the support of other members. Some people would argue that their resistance is itself due to prior brainwashing on the part of those involved. But this is only calling the process by another name. Brainwashing works so effectively because, through their total environmental control, interrogators are able to make everything in personal experience fit the new story. For novice Jehovah's Witnesses, for young men passing through army officer training – for these people too, everything in their daily lives acts to support and confirm the special beliefs, the special status, which they hold along with the comrades around them. The strength of this social identity, its resistance to the deliberate personal assault of brainwashing, is the strength of a personal story intimately shared, deeply reinforced, among the members of a select social institution whose reach extends back through history.

As the techniques of brainwashing show, to change our personal stories is to change our lives. The metaphor of life as natural cycle views change as the unfolding of a pre-existing, unalterable human nature, and, consequently, reifies the current status quo as natural and right. In the metaphor of life as story, human practices are not fixed, are, potentially, open to infinite variation. It is because we tell ourselves certain kinds of story that we come to do things in particular ways, to give our lives the particular forms they take. Yet though, in this metaphor, the most far-reaching, the most profound changes are possible in human life, this does not mean that they are easy.

Many people are deeply dissatisfied with the chief character in their life story. You find yourself to be a prison within which you are trapped. The wretched personality who seems to be you is someone you would gladly escape from, if you could. Yet somehow this is impossible. Time and again you re-enter the all-too-familiar vicious circles, react in the same disastrous ways. And this gives your story a terrible repetitiveness. Thinking to start a fresh chapter, in new surroundings, you make the same mistakes all over again. Your second marriage, which seemed at first so different from the other, somehow acquires an identical pattern, founders in the very same way. How is it that, despite the bitter lessons life has taught you, the passionate resolutions you have made, you are still stuck in the same groove, destined, it seems, to play out the same disasters for as long as you live?

In principle, each of us could do anything. Like Luke Rinehart's dice man, we could select how we chose to act from a huge range of possibilities, simply according to the throw of a dice. But of course to do this would be to enter personal chaos, for it would mean that we had to jettison the story which gives meaning, predictability, continuity to our lives. And in any story, the character of the protagonist is absolutely crucial. The novel we read is, in the end, convincing or unconvincing according to whether we can believe in the characterization. Would that kind of person do that, feel that, react like that? In living, we can maintain the credibility of our life story only if we continue to act in character. And it is because we ourselves cannot envisage how we could sustain our own character, were we to step outside our habitual, familiar ways of behaving, that we do, so often, find ourselves trapped.

Drastic changes in character are, of course, possible if you begin a new story altogether. In adolescence, people sometimes try to do this; nothing of the repudiated former child is acknowledged within the new, grown-up person who stands there. Sometimes adults, too, tell life stories which have no continuity with the story of their childish lives. Their present story does not begin until much later – has its origins in settings more like the ones they now inhabit. There is a strangeness about these stories, which seem truncated and lacking in depth. The advertising tycoon, Peter Marsh, talking to Anthony Clare, alone among the series of interviewees, strongly denied any personal roots in childhood.* His vehement protests, that his constant striving to

---

* Clare, A., *In the Psychiatrist's Chair*, Chatto & Windus, 1984.

shine, as an adult, owed nothing to his childish experience of
being paraded as a boy wonder by his mother, seemed ultimately
unconvincing. The story suggested by the psychiatrist was, in
this case, easier to believe than was the protagonist's own story.
The same lack of credibility is, perhaps, generally felt by those
who witness personal 'rebirths'. The radical changes in life-style,
relationships, concerns, undertaken by those who are 'reborn'
within the philosophy of a fanatical sect, may not always disguise
from sceptical friends and family the person they have always
known.

To change the story of our lives must, in fact, always involve
changes for other people. Because our stories must have an
audience, because their themes encompass other lives besides our
own, because our characters are intimately, inextricably inter-
linked – we cannot, as single individuals, take the story just
wherever we might choose. Arbitrarily to introduce a radical new
departure in your personal story is to interrupt the dance, to
court the protest, or the disbelief, of others. Changes that are
convincing, that can be personally lived out, can only be made
jointly with others.

In our own society, the women's movement does, perhaps,
illuminate much of what it means to change the story of our lives.
Unlike those who, in their rebirths, attempt sudden drastic
changes in character, in personal story, members of the women's
movement do not try to repudiate the story that has been told so
far. Instead, through the delicate, intuitive work of conscious-
ness-raising, women listen carefully to each other's stories, follow
as sensitively as they can the form that each plot takes. Only
through careful attention to the details of a life story does it
become possible to construct, together, its deeper personal
meanings, its wider social ramifications. And in such work, the
essential intertwining, the complementarity, of characters, of
stories, becomes evident. A change in character, in the part that
an individual plays in her story, demands that reciprocal changes
be made in other characters, other stories. For many women in
such groups, it becomes possible to envision what kinds of
changes might be made. By tracing, in intimate detail, how the

story has developed so far, further, credible developments may sometimes be imagined. And these developments may begin to be lived out within the women's groups themselves, where rules of inter-relating have come to be very different from those operating generally in our society.

To create a life story which is credible, which allows development as well as continuity, which tells a tale worth telling – this is the task that, as human beings, we must all attempt. It is a task which, essentially, demands imagination. If we are to construct a coherent account – an account which encompasses, rather than denies, all the phases we have lived through, the vicissitudes, the pain as well as the joy – then we must approach our experience, and that of others, with the greatest possible imagination. It is only through our imaginative construction that we shall be able to own the full heritage of the experience we have acquired through living in time. And if we are to affirm the meaning, the value, of our own story, we must make an act of personal faith. In the end, it is the storyteller who, like any novelist, commands the audience. Our sense of the meaning of our story – that is our contribution to life.

INDEX OF NAMES

INDEX OF SUBJECTS